WILDLIFE
HEROES

40 Leading Conservationists and the Animals They Are Committed to Saving

by Julie Scardina and Jeff Flocken

with Photo Editor Sterling Zumbrunn

RUNNING PRESS
PHILADELPHIA · LONDON

Books published by Running Press are available at special discounts for bulk purchases in the United States by corporations, institutions, and other organizations. For more information, please contact the Special Markets Department at the Perseus Books Group, 2300 Chestnut Street, Suite 200, Philadelphia, PA 19103, or call (800) 810-4145, ext. 5000, or e-mail special.markets@perseusbooks.com.

ISBN 978-0-7624-4319-2
Library of Congress Control Number: 2011939378

E-book ISBN 978-0-7624-4516-5

9 8 7 6 5 4 3 2 1
Digit on the right indicates the number of this printing

Photo Editor Sterling Zumbrunn

Cover and interior design by Jason Kayser
Typography: Mercury and Proxima Nova

Running Press Book Publishers
2300 Chestnut Street
Philadelphia, PA 19103-4371

Visit us on the web!
www.runningpress.com

CONTENTS

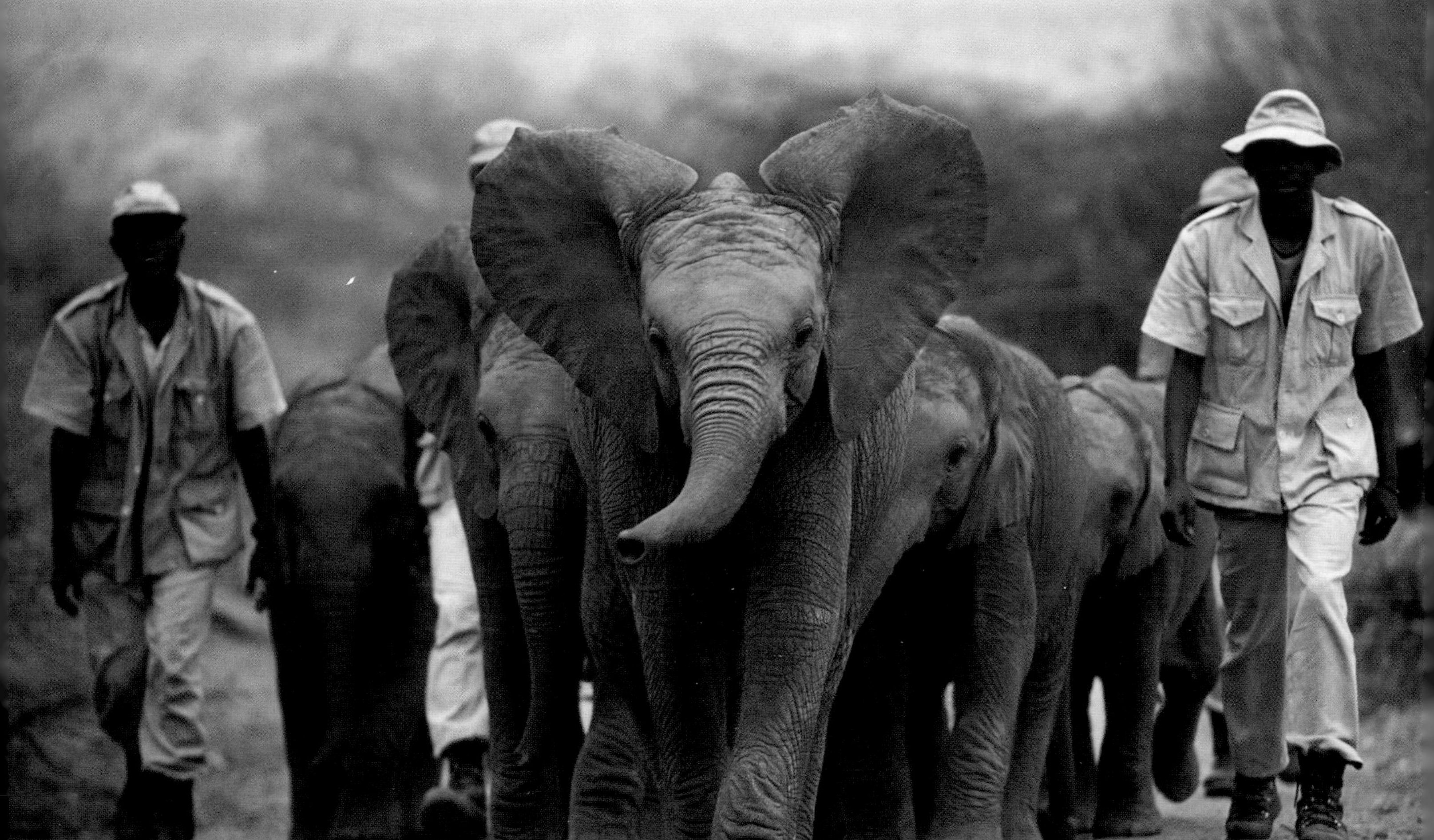

INTRODUCTION

The wildlife heroes featured in this book are forty individuals we admire and respect—acclaimed for their vision, determination, and success. Some of them we have known for many years and worked closely with, while others we only knew before this book through knowledge of their impressive accomplishments, or from their stellar reputations in the field of wildlife conservation.

Admittedly, the assemblage of species we chose to highlight show a bias of the authors, as we have our own personal love for certain animals and direct experiences working in particular conservation arenas. So while we both have great fondness for critters like the obscure dwarf wedgemussel and the underrated dung beetle, and understand their important roles in their habitats, this book tends to feature the big charismatic species, the same ones who rightly or wrongly tend to receive the most conservation resources and public attention. Luckily these same high-profile animals frequently serve vital roles as keystone, flagship, and indicator species, thereby arguably deserving the lion's share of adoration they receive.

These individual species, like the heroes selected for the book, were also chosen as being best suited to bring a broader message of conservation need, and inspiration for action, to readers. We are compelled to feature these heroes, species and issues as we both feel the heartbreak of what is happening to the wild animals and wild places we love. Unless more people help fight the war we are currently losing to save species, wild lands, and ocean habitats, there will be far less of these incredible creatures and environments left in the world.

The heroes in this book have dedicated their lives to preserving these creatures; animals that are beloved by the world because they are both compelling and fascinating. We are proud to shine a light on them all. And we sincerely hope that this book will result in more support for the heroes' critical efforts and in meaningful gains in the struggle for existence of these amazing species.

Julie Scardina and Jeff Flocken

EARTH

WORKING ON THE GROUND

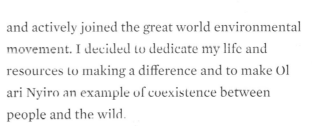

BY KUKI GALLMAN, ACCLAIMED AUTHOR OF *I DREAMED OF AFRICA*, ENVIRONMENTAL ACTIVIST, AND FOUNDER OF THE GALLMAN AFRICA CONSERVANCY

Caring for Eden

It was about forty years ago that I moved to Kenya and acquired the responsibility to look after a piece of heaven on the Eastern Great Rift Valley, Ol ari Nyiro, a biodiversity oasis of rugged, dramatic landscapes, with a relic forest and natural springs, gorges, and ravines, where endemic species of wildlife and flora survived and still do, in stark contrast with the now degraded landscape surrounding us, from where most indigenous vegetation has been removed.

In the very early '80s, after the tragic deaths of both my husband and my son within a short space of time, witnessing the tragic environmental degradation and loss of habitat and species occurring all around Kenya, I resisted attempts from friends and family to get me to abandon Ol ari Nyiro to its destiny and return to my native Italy, and actively joined the great world environmental movement. I decided to dedicate my life and resources to making a difference and to make Ol ari Nyiro an example of coexistence between people and the wild.

I became a Kenya citizen and a spokesperson for my adopted country on matters of environment, and transformed the place from an operating livestock ranch into a nature conservancy with no domestic stock, where all life is nurtured and protected.

What was happening at that time? With the collapse of Somalia and deserters from that country's army infiltrating the northern parts of Kenya—their only wealth their weapons—the killing of rhino and elephants became an unprecedented issue in Kenya, and, having lost nine black indigenous rhinoceros in Ol ari Nyiro in less than one year, I decided to do something about it. I started the first private antipoaching unit in Kenya.

What was beginning to happen—and has happened since—all around us, and throughout Africa and the planet, is the drastic restriction in wildlife habitat, pressures of all kinds due mostly to population increase, change of land use from pastoral to agricultural land, consequent interruption of migratory routes, deforestation, pollution, overgrazing, erosion, siltage in lakes, climate change with subsequent droughts, lack of job opportunities for growing populations of tribal youth and the concurrent growth of demand for wildlife products in the surging markets of the Far East, insecurity, tribal conflicts, and, in Kenya, the proliferation of small weapons from the troubled neighborhood of Somalia and the Sudan.

This, in conjunction with the soaring black markets stimulated throughout the Continent as a consequence of the sales of ivory allowed by CITES in 2007, after the twenty-year moratorium in all sales initiated by the ivory fire in Kenya in 1989, has signified an increase in poaching and illegal trade of animal body parts throughout the continent of Africa, and in particular from elephants, rhino, lions, snakes (pythons), tortoises, in addition to leopards, and plants—African sandalwood, a once-common shrub, has become rare—just to mention the most dramatic and tangible species loss. As an honorary game warden with the Kenya Wildlife Service, I have committed to do all in my capacity to fight the illegal trade that is at the root of the cruel and senseless killings that I witness continuously in the African bush.

The commitment to active conservation of the wild parts and inhabitants of our Earth demands time, stamina, vision, dedication, and daring. It can be dangerous, but in my case, despite several physical attacks (one of which crippled my left hand) and endless threats, this is one battle that I am determined to keep fighting with all the means at my disposal since I passionately believe in our responsibility to protect what has never been easier to destroy.

I am honored to introduce this impressive list of wildlife heroes, all leaders in their chosen fields, men and women of extraordinary expertise, talent, and courage, who spend and often risk their lives in the front line of conservation in remote and often lonely parts of our planet, to ensure that today's species will not become tomorrow's dinosaurs.

Your contribution is incalculable, and with deep respect and gratitude, I salute you.

GREG RASMUSSEN
AFRICAN PAINTED DOG

"Learning about [their] loyal behavior has made a big impression on both those who work with African painted dogs and even those who previously hated the dogs, but now are willing to share their land with them."

African Painted Dog

→ **Scientific Name:** *Lycaon pictus*

→ **Range:** Painted dogs formerly occupied a wide range of habitats throughout sub-Saharan Africa; however, they are now extirpated from 25 of 39 former range states.

→ **Population Trend:** Declining. There are an estimated 3,000 to 5,500 painted dogs left on the entire African continent.

→ **IUCN* Status:** Endangered

*IUCN here and elsewhere stands for the International Union for Conservation of Nature.

Gregory Rasmussen

→ **Education:** PhD from Oxford University, United Kingdom

→ **Nationality:** British

→ **Organizational Affiliation:** Painted Dog Conservation

→ **Years Working with African Painted Dogs:** 24

→ **Honors:** Whitley Wildinvest Continuation Award for Conservation (2001); Wildlife Society Annual Award (2000); Whitley Runner-up Award for Conservation (1999); and Research on Ocean Currents in the Atlantic (1978)

→ **Notable Accomplishments:** Appointed to the IUCN/SSC Canid Specialist Group; selected to join North and South Poles Transglobe Expedition; founded the Painted Dog Conservation organization; named a Wildlife Conservation Network partner; helped double the African painted dog population in Zimbabwe

GREG Rasmussen hates the name many people have given his favorite animals. "They are not simply 'wild' dogs; they are not feral domesticated canines with which people confuse them because of their name. When people know nothing about them, they fear them. Instead," Rasmussen counters, "they are beautiful and endangered 'painted dogs' which need our understanding and assistance if they are going to continue to survive in Africa."

Rasmussen is particularly sensitive about misperceptions of these social and wide-ranging canines—known not only as African wild dogs and painted dogs but also as "African hunting dogs," "Cape hunting dogs," and "spotted dogs." "When my mother first read about the animals I was intent on studying many years ago," he says, "she was fearful for my life, as there were so many awful and false descriptions of the dogs in books she read." Today those myths carry on in many of the animal's range countries. "Most people grow up being told to shoot the dogs on sight because they think they are cruel, bloodthirsty, savage, and no good to anyone."

Rasmussen started working with painted dogs in 1989, when he was overwhelmed by the

What You Should Know about African Painted Dogs

→ Painted dogs are not domesticated dogs that have run wild, but rather a distinct species that evolved separately from other canids. Their scientific name translated from Latin means "painted wolflike animal."

→ Between 43 and 70 percent of wild dog hunts end in success compared to lesser success rates of many other predators, such as lions, which are successful only an estimated 27 to 32 percent of the time.

→ Painted dogs have been shown to mourn for deceased pack members.

→ The loss of just one adult pack member—whether to a snare, a vehicle, or a gunshot—can spell doom for the entire pack, as every dog is needed to hunt and protect the pups.

→ Painted dogs allow pups to feed first after a kill and will bring food back to any pack member that, due to injury, illness, or "babysitting duties," cannot participate.

human-induced carnage to this highly endangered species. "No sooner than I had identified the presence of this rare animal did I find that shortly afterwards, they had momentarily left the sanctuary of the national park and were either shot by ranchers, killed on the road, or caught in poachers' snares set for bushmeat. These senseless mortalities distressed me deeply, and so I decided to make the species my flagship in the hope of 'making a difference.'" He started with neither funding nor accommodation and precious few savings, and he was distrusted by just about everyone—the local Africans, ranchers, and even safari operators who did not recognize the dogs' potential value. Winning confidences—without falling off the track—became the issue.

To combat this, he started a major awareness campaign alerting people to the truths about the species and the problems they faced. Rasmussen's vehicle, which also served as his home in the beginning, frequently touched ranchland areas where it was not welcome, and he was seen as much a problem as the dogs themselves. Rasmussen and his programs became a point of vociferous public discussion. He recalls being delighted at receiving a call from a rancher who said he was going to "bury him" because the dogs had expanded to the point that they were now on his ranch and Rasmussen was "responsible." The very fact that he called said one thing; the fact that the dogs had expanded into a new area said even more. Years before, the rancher would simply have killed the dogs and not considered calling. Rasmussen translocated the animals to a safer area, thus demonstrating his ability and willingness to do whatever was necessary to keep them alive.

A decade after Rasmussen started his painted dog work, Zimbabwe overnight became a turbulent mix of conflict, lawlessness, increased poverty, and starvation, and once again African painted dogs were in jeopardy. Snaring, a technique using wire to catch animals for meat and sale, hit astronomical proportions, and painted dogs often fell victim to these death traps. All the gains of the previous years were threatened. It was back to the drawing board for Rasmussen, though this time accompanied by Peter Blinston, who came from the UK to "help out" for a few months and ended up staying on. In a climate where few locals had much to rely on, the tenacity of the project carried through and the Painted Dog Conservation project (PDC) was expanded to include the community as partners.

As conservation ignorance is Rasmussen's greatest enemy, the program of which he is most proud is the organization's Children's Bush Camp. The effort introduces local kids to native wildlife, as well as to the dogs at the PDC rescue center. "Zimbabwe children, as in many other countries, often never get the chance to experience or learn positive things about wildlife in their own nation. Once they do, they are forever changed," relates Rasmussen. The children attend classes, perform skits, write reports, and visit Hwange National Park to see animals in the wild. The kids even get a "surprise" encounter with the normally elusive painted dogs by taking a nature walk down a long, raised walkway through the rescued dogs' enclosure right before feeding time. The dogs are then released and come running toward their meal, right beneath where the children are standing, to their complete thrill and astonishment.

Painted dogs used to regularly roam over much of Africa, their range extending to thirty-nine countries. Now there are estimated to be fewer than fifty-five hundred painted dogs in all of Africa. Shooting, snares, and road strikes are the major threats, and the Painted Dog Conservation program

is busy addressing them all. Besides education, there are concrete, practical solutions that can save individual dogs' lives. For example, PDC places wide, spiked, reflective collars on dogs, which serve multiple purposes.

First, they can aid in freeing the dogs. The spikes on these collars help break or prevent tightening of snare wire, often placed to catch other game animals, but sometimes catching dogs instead when they investigate the bait. Reflective material on the collars helps warn drivers of dogs crossing the road at night. The collars also double as radio transmitters, helping to keep track of packs and their movements and add to the body of knowledge about these misunderstood animals. Coupled with road signs at common dog crossing points, radio collaring has reduced road mortality by 50 percent.

PDC is a popular employer of locals, who find careers as dog keepers, educators, researchers, anti-poaching patrol team members, bus drivers, facility maintenance workers, and cooks. "It has made a difference that we are a relatively stable provider during some of the worst economic times the country has ever seen," Rasmussen says. "We take care of the dogs and the people."

PDC has become somewhat of a regional phenomenon. Neighboring communities are impressed with the work Rasmussen has accomplished, and the dogs' reputation has improved. "People around here are now telling us when they see dogs in the wild, and if someone finds an injured one—by car collision or snare, they will often alert us so we can try to save the dog."

This lesson in compassion can be learned from the dogs themselves. When a pack member is injured, the rest of the pack, adults and pups alike, will take care of it, bring it food, and lick its wounds until it has recovered. "Learning about that loyal behavior has made a big impression on both those who work with African painted dogs and those who previously hated them, but now are willing to share their land with them."

In 2003, Rasmussen found himself in a dire situation when he crashed his plane while helping the National Parks Service look for a rhino. Since he crashed outside of the search area, he spent more than twenty-four hours in the wilderness with broken legs, ankles, and pelvis before help arrived. The crash was made legendary by the retelling both in a Discovery Channel documentary and on a television series called *Alive*. Rasmussen has recovered, but is forbidden by his friends and associates to ever fly again. Many would have quit working in the bush after such a terrifying near-death experience. But Rasmussen remains committed to the painted dogs and their future survival. "Painted dogs have increased from just 350 to 700 animals in Zimbabwe since we started our programs twenty years ago. My colleagues and I have faced many challenges along the way—but the news is positive overall. Whether you call them painted dogs, African hunting dogs, or spotted dogs—there are more around today than there were when I started working with them, and that's a great sign for their future!"

Why It Is Important To Save African Painted Dogs

Painted dogs are the only living representative of a distinct line of wolflike species of a lineage several million years old. This genetic uniqueness is very valuable to biodiversity.

BELINDA LOW
GREVY'S ZEBRA

"It was only when I started working with them that I understood the magnitude of their decline. I didn't want these beautiful animals to disappear from my homeland."

FAST FACTS

Grevy's Zebra

→ **Scientific Name:** *Equus grevyi*

→ **Range:** This species was once found throughout most of Kenya, Eritrea, Ethiopia, and Somalia but is now found only in northern Kenya and isolated pockets in Ethiopia.

→ **Population Trend:** Considered stable now due to protection and conservation efforts. It is estimated that fewer than 3,000 Grevy's zebras are left in the wild.

→ **IUCN Status:** Endangered

Belinda Low

→ **Education:** Master's from Durrell Institute of Conservation and Ecology, University of Kent, United Kingdom

→ **Nationality:** Kenyan and British

→ **Organizational Affiliation:** Grevy's Zebra Trust

→ **Years Working with Grevy's Zebras:** 10

→ **Notable Accomplishments:** Founded the Grevy's Zebra Scout Programme; developed the Northern Rangelands Endangered Species Program; certified educator in holistic management used to improve habitat deterioration; founding member of Kenya's Grevy's Zebra Task Force

BELINDA Low, born and raised in Kenya, has nearly always regarded the Grevy's zebra as one of the most spectacular large animals on the planet—and for good reason. It is striking, powerful, unique, and endangered.

Kenya is home to 95 percent of Grevy's zebras, but it wasn't until after Low began studying this limited-range species that they became her passion and focus. "It was only when I started working with them that I understood the magnitude of their decline. I didn't want these beautiful animals to disappear from my homeland," she says. "I had to do something."

Low works as much with the people who share the same land and resources of Grevy's zebras as she does with the zebras themselves. Where the zebras range in northern Kenya, people are mainly pastoralists. As keepers of livestock, they have an intrinsic knowledge of nature that has served them well for centuries; life-giving rain supplied regularly twice a year has helped them and the animals survive on the arid land. But things are changing. The rains are no longer predictable—or often, as plentiful. "The future of these peoples' livelihoods and the survival of the Grevy's zebra are inextricably linked."

Today, Low is teaching a low-tech method of range management using the same cattle that once competed with the zebras, but now help till and enrich the soil and restore native grasses for wildlife. Cattle are kept in smaller but mobile grazing areas to rid selected zones of invasive grasses. In the process, the cattle provide natural fertilizer and a churning of the Earth by their hooves. Once

indigestible, tough grasses are eaten to the root and tramped down, native seeds can naturally take hold. "Cattle allowed to roam widely don't provide benefits for indigenous plants and therefore the wildlife," says Low. "It's when cattle are concentrated that improvements can occur, and that's actually pretty easy to do. It's such a simple concept and an all-around winning situation for locals, wildlife, and the environment. We just need to reach a lot more communities to set up these management systems."

Low works across an area of more than ten thousand square kilometers (approximately sixty-two hundred square miles), transected by a huge mountain range. "We camp whenever we are away from the field headquarters, which gives us great opportunities to interact directly with the locals," she says. "Some of the most significant conversations have taken place around the campfire!" As difficult as the terrain and the zebra's challenges are, Low enjoys the work and the relationships she has built with her neighbors. She has worked to set up task forces and national strategies to ensure community commitment and long-term support for the Grevy's zebra. "We must recognize the critical role

What You Should Know about Zebras

→ Newborn zebra foals are ready to run with the herd just an hour or two after birth—a critical survival capability for an African prey animal.

→ There are three species of zebra. The plains zebra of the famous Serengeti migration is the only one whose populations are not of concern.

→ The mountain zebra is listed as vulnerable, with an estimated total population of 9,000 adults.

→ The Grevy's zebra population is estimated to have declined by more than 50 percent in just the past two decades.

→ The Grevy's zebra is the largest member of the wild equid family and unlike other zebra species, resembles a mule more than a horse, with a narrow head and fuzzy, oversized ears.

Why It Is Important to Save Grevy's Zebras

Zebras are a primary consumer of the grasslands—they consume the coarse, dryer, longer blades, actually stimulating new grass growth by clipping it shorter, providing more tender new shoots for other herbivores. Grevy's zebras have adapted to live in dryer regions than the other two zebra species—providing expanded ranges for zebra predators, such as lions and hyenas. By saving Grevy's zebras many other wildlife species living in the same landscape are also protected, as well as the ancient culture of the livestock-herding people inhabiting the region.

the local pastoral people play in the Grevy's zebra's survival," she says, "and help them manage the entire ecosystem effectively for all its inhabitants."

Grevy's zebras have a totally different social system than the more numerous plains zebra, which served them well in their ecological niche until resources and numbers began to decline. Breeding males remain on their territories year-round—sometimes even in times of severe drought. Females and nonterritorial (bachelor) males will migrate to more habitable pastures. As fewer than three thousand Grevy's zebras remain over thousands of square kilometers in northern Kenya and Ethiopia, the strongest, most territorial males are often left with a territory no females traverse. On top of habitat loss, water shortages, hunting pressures and human disturbance, this certainly makes a successful breeding season more difficult, so the downward population spiral continues.

In order to work more closely with the people who share the zebra's landscape, Low started the Grevy's Zebra Trust, employing men and women from the local communities to help monitor the zebra. This, along with education programs and cattle herdsmen recognizing that the zebras can not only help them find water and suitable grazing land but also alert them to the presence of predators, has put the zebra back in good standing and given the species a fighting chance.

Low's undergraduate degree is in Hispanic studies, which she discovered in college and fell in love with. It led her to Bolivia, an amazingly diverse bioregion that rekindled her early love for wildlife and conservation. "I met people who inspired me to follow those dreams," says Low. "That led to my master's degree in conservation biology and my future with Grevy's zebra. Now I still get to read Hispanic literature when I want, but more meaningfully to me, I am devoting myself to helping the Grevy's zebra survive. I am possibly the luckiest person on Earth."

CLAUDINE ANDRÉ
BONOBO

"Ever since I nursed that first baby bonobo back to health all those years ago, I knew that these animals would be part of my life."

Bonobo

→ **Scientific Name:** *Pan paniscus*

→ **Range:** Bonobos are only found in forested areas of the Democratic Republic of the Congo, Africa.

→ **Population Trend:** Prolonged warfare in the region has made studying bonobos extremely difficult; however, bonobos are thought to have experienced significant declines over the past thirty years.

→ **IUCN Status:** Endangered

Claudine André

→ **Education:** State's Women Superior Technical School, Charleroi, Belgium

→ **Nationality:** Belgian

→ **Organizational Affiliation:** Lola ya Bonobo Sanctuary

→ **Years Working with Bonobos:** 19

→ **Honors:** Badham-Evans Award for Women in Conservation (2008); awarded the National Order of Merit by France (2006); Prince Laurent Prize of the Environment by Belgium (2006)

→ **Books Published:** *Wild Tenderness: My Paradise for Bonobos in the Heart of Africa*

→ **Notable Accomplishments:** Founded Les Amis des Bonobo du Congo and Lola ya Bonobo Sanctuary, the world's first bonobo sanctuary; organized the first-ever successful reintroduction of bonobos back into the wild

WITH no formal education in primatology or any other animal science, Belgium-born Claudine André is an unexpected candidate to achieve landmark accomplishments for one of the great ape species—but that is exactly what she has done. Along with her colleagues at the Lola ya Bonobo Sanctuary—which means "Bonobo Paradise" in Lingala, the main language in the Democratic Republic of the Congo (DRC), where the sanctuary is located—André successfully reintroduced the first-ever troop of rehabilitated bonobos into the wild in 2009. This tremendous feat is just one in a string of inspiring achievements in André's compelling life story.

When she was three years old, André moved to the DRC with her veterinarian father. She grew up surrounded by jungle and wildness, which made an indelible impression on her. "Nature became part of my everyday world, and it shaped my values and aspirations."

After completing her schooling back in Belgium, she returned to the DRC, raised five children near the shadow of the Virunga volcano, and finally moved to Kinshasa in 1978. However, in 1993 her life took a new turn when she was brought a sickly, orphaned bonobo while volunteering at the Kinshasa Zoo. Despite being told that all bonobos that came to the zoo from the wild invariably died, André committed herself to saving the infant, and much to everyone's surprise, it survived. Once word got out that there was a woman who could save bonobos, local people began bringing injured and orphaned bonobos to Claudine. With a home for orphaned bonobos now available, officials from the DRC Ministry of the Environment began confiscating captive bonobos, whose capture and sale are illegal by Congolese law. To address the growing demand, André started the not-for-profit Les Amis des Bonobos du Congo (ABC) and opened a bonobo nursery affiliated with the American School of Kinshasa.

In 2002 André took her efforts one step further and opened Lola ya Bonobo, the world's first bonobo sanctuary. Located on a seventy-acre enclosed forest outside of Kinshasa, the refuge includes three separate enclosures and night buildings, as well as its own nursery. "Ever since I nursed that first baby bonobo back to health all those years ago," says André, "I knew that these animals would be part of my life. I just keep looking for the next big thing I can do to help them, and there is always something. They are a species in need of assistance."

Sometimes called "the forgotten apes" or "pygmy chimpanzees," bonobos are found exclusively in the DRC, and along with the chimpanzee are considered the closest living relative of humans. Bonobos are less studied and lesser known than the other great apes—orangutans, gorillas, and chimpanzees. And while bonobos and chimpanzees are

very similar in appearance, they have a number of distinguishing differences. Bonobos tend to have longer limbs, a thinner build, dark faces, and pink lips. But the most important differences between bonobos and chimpanzees involve their psychology. Unlike chimpanzees, bonobos are a female-dominated society. They engage in very little hunting and no war. Most important, no bonobo has ever been seen to kill another bonobo. Peace is maintained in the group through sexual contact and play.

The Lola ya Bonobo Sanctuary and ABC not only offer much-needed help to individual bonobos, but they also look to address the larger problem endangering the species. Only ten thousand to forty thousand bonobos are left in the wild, with less than a quarter of their natural habitat intact. They are typically brought to the sanctuary as collateral damage from the long, ongoing civil strife in the

What You Should Know about Bonobos

→ The dominant individual in a bonobo group is always a female.

→ Sexual activity among bonobos is used as a bonding tool and a means for keeping peace.

→ Unlike chimpanzees, which communicate in low-pitched, guttural noises, bonobos use high-pitched vocalizations to communicate.

→ Bonobos and humans share more than 98 percent of the same genetic makeup.

→ Bonobos do not war, and no bonobo has ever been seen to kill another.

DRC. Decades of conflict have left locals lacking basic needs. As a result, they frequently turn to the jungle for food and resources. When this happens, bonobos are often left orphans after their parents are killed illegally for bushmeat, or infants are taken from the wild for the pet trade and later confiscated by officials who have no means to care for them.

André and her colleagues work to educate Congolese youth, law enforcement officers, government officials, and local decision makers about bonobos and the need to protect them. These efforts focus on improving existing wildlife trade and enforcement laws and reducing demand for bushmeat. The sanctuary's education programs reach more than thirty thousand Congolese each year, most of them schoolchildren. André and her team have also started reaching out directly to hunters and bushmeat traders in local markets to try to stop the trade at its source. All this is done in addition to their ongoing efforts to provide a safe, comfortable environment for orphaned and injured bonobos brought to the sanctuary.

Unfortunately, while the sanctuary has been able to take in these at-risk apes and provide safety and medical treatment for almost ten years, it has only finite resources and space. Working within these limitations, André strove for years to develop and implement a plan for reintroducing a troop of rescued bonobos into the wild. The reintroduction not only provided an opportunity for individual bonobos to live a more natural existence in the wild, it also offered the chance to increase genetic diversity in wild populations and reestablish bonobos in regions where they have been wiped out.

To prepare for this reintroduction, André and her team had to identify a safe location suitable for bonobo habitat but devoid of a current population so as not to inadvertently spread disease or cause territorial conflict. After finding a site where bonobos once lived but had not been seen for decades, André began negotiating with stakeholders at both the release site and at the

Why It Is Important to Save Bonobos

Bonobos help shape the forest thru foraging, hunting, and seed dispersal. They also serve to "trim" vegetation and to control termite and other insect numbers. Finally, they show that it is possible for hominids to live without war. If bonobos go extinct, there will be no way for researchers to discover the exact mechanisms by which human's closest living relatives live in peace.

national level, to build support for the project on the ground, and to ensure that all required authorizations were obtained. All the released bonobos would be protected in the twenty-thousand-hectare forest (almost eighty square miles). Local residents, the Ilonga Pôo, agreed to become their guardians. In return, ABC supplied educational materials for five primary schools and two secondary schools, benefiting more than a thousand students. The schools had not had new material since the 1980s. ABC supplied blackboards, writing tablets, and updated textbooks for every classroom. The nonprofit also provided the community a start-up stock of essential medicines that can be purchased at the village pharmacy, at cost.

Finally, André had to ensure that the best-suited bonobos were identified for the reintroduction and that appropriate measures were in place to monitor the project's success and the health of the individual animals before, during, and after the release.

"Reintroduction is complicated and can be a disaster for both the individual animals being brought back to the forest and for the wild populations if it is done wrong," says André. "There is so much riding on doing it right the first time that we couldn't afford to make any mistakes."

While many of the bonobos at the sanctuary have been there too long or have injuries that would prevent them from successfully reentering the wild, some were viable candidates for reintroduction. After clearing health protocols, selection and translocation guidelines, and site requirements; monitoring behavior; searching for local bonobo populations; hiring vets and community outreach teams; and acquiring seemingly endless government permits, André released nine bonobos into the wild for the first time ever attempted. The troop included two pregnant bonobos, who have since successfully given birth in the wild. This reintroduction will serve as a model for future introductions—the next of which is already being planned—and a source of hope that bonobos can still survive in the world.

"Having done this shows the world that conservationists, the Congolese people, and governments can all work together to make room for wild animals," says André. "And I can't think of a more incredible species to find a place for in the wild than bonobos. The truly remarkable forgotten ape—which maybe with a little luck won't end up being forgotten after all."

ROGÉRIO CUNHA DE PAULA
MANED WOLF

"Anytime I can help these incredible animals, it makes me proud to be doing what I do every day."

FAST FACTS

Maned Wolf

→ **Scientific Name:** *Chrysocyon brachyurus*

→ **Range:** Central South America, including the countries of Argentina, Bolivia, Brazil, Paraguay, Peru, and Uruguay

→ **Population Trend:** Habitat loss, hunting pressures, persecution due to conflicts, and road kills are all negatively impacting maned wolf populations.

→ **IUCN Status:** Near Threatened

Rogério Cunha de Paula

→ **Education:** Master's degree from Florida Atlantic University

→ **Nationality:** Brazilian

→ **Organizational Affiliation:** Instituto Pro-Carnivoros; Brazilian Agency for Biodiversity Conservation (ICMBio) through the National Research Center for Carnivores Conservation (CENAP)

→ **Years Working with Maned Wolves:** 14

→ **Books Published:** *Serra da Canastra,* written with his wife, Laís Duarte Mota.

→ **Notable Accomplishments:** Extensive work to help protect Serra da Canastra National Park, which has one of the highest maned wolf populations in Brazil but is threatened by development and encroaching human populations

ROGÉRIO Cunha de Paula is a Brazilian biologist with an intense love for carnivores, and a passion for the maned wolf in particular. He first began working with the species in 1998, and has since become the preeminent expert on these creatures.

"Maned wolves are amazing—they have these bizarre radar dish–like ears, rust-colored fur, and crazy, black-socked, stilt legs," notes de Paula, "You'd think they would be incredibly awkward and obvious in the savannah where they live, but instead they have evolved perfectly to succeed in their natural environment."

The species' long legs allow them to move effortlessly through the tall grass savannahs where they tend to live, and their oversized ears enable them to hear small rodents and prey scurrying in the underbrush. And while they are well suited for hunting small birds and mammals, they also eat fruit and as a result fill an important niche as seed dispersers in the grasslands, or "cerrado," region.

Maned wolves are currently battling the pressure of habitat loss due to expanding agriculture and human sprawl. These phenomena have also contributed to escalating conflict between humans and maned wolves—the latter of which is not above occasionally poaching a chicken from a yard.

What You Should Know about Maned Wolves

→ About half of the maned wolf's diet is made up of fruits and plant matter, and the other half is composed of small and medium-sized animals, such as rodents, birds, lizards, snakes, and armadillos.

→ Maned wolves are highly adapted to live in the grasslands where they are found, with long, thin legs and an acute sense of hearing useful for moving and hunting in savannah grasses.

→ Domestic dogs are a threat to maned wolves in that they spread disease to the wolves, compete with them for food, and have been known to attack them.

→ Maned wolves are the primary seed disperser for the *fruta-do-lobo*, or "wolf's fruit," another name for the wolf apple common in Brazil.

Why It Is Important to Save Maned Wolves

As opportunistic omnivores, maned wolves not only help control animal populations lower down the food chain, but they also have a role as seed dispersers.

de Paula has developed education plans and creative solutions to stop persecution of maned wolves by locals who now share their territory. Wolf-proof chicken coops have been one of the successful tools he has introduced to stop the conflict, and as a result, both wolves and chickens are doing better these days in the areas where he works.

"Anytime I can help these incredible animals, it makes me proud to be doing what I do every day," says de Paula, "and that includes helping the chickens too."

de Paula works in Serra da Canastra National Park, which is a thirteen-hour drive from his home in São Paulo, Brazil. This park is one of the best places on Earth to see not only maned wolves, but giant anteaters as well. One time while filming a lounging maned wolf, de Paula did a 360-degree pan of the landscape and was able to film five different anteaters in a single rotation—all within a few hundred yards of where he was standing.

Unfortunately, the large national park where he works is threatened by logging, mining operations, and conversion of habitat for soy plantations—all of which are being encouraged by the government of Brazil to promote economic development. de Paula is campaigning to have the park's private land, where these activities are currently happening, converted into public land and restored to their natural state. Without such a plan, the park will eventually be so fragmented that all the wildlife within it could be compromised and eventually lost.

Besides the maned wolf and the park's natural beauty, Serra da Canastra has special meaning for de Paula—he met his wife, Laís, a Brazilian television reporter, when she came out to interview him in the park about his work. She now joins him regularly for his trips to do research at Serra da Canastra.

"The park and the maned wolf are an important part of our life together," says de Paula. "We were married here, and we hope to bring our children here one day. And when they visit, we want them to see the wolves. And the giant anteaters. And all the beauty of Serra da Canastra. It needs to be part of their future, and we will do everything we can to make sure it is preserved for them."

JOHN LUKAS
OKAPI

"Okapis have evolved to perfectly blend into the forest—I've never actually seen a wild okapi in all my years working to conserve them."

John Lukas

→ **Education:** Master's degree from Northeastern University, Massachusetts

→ **Nationality:** American

→ **Organizational Affiliation:** Okapi Conservation Project

→ **Years Working with Okapis:** 25

→ **Notable Accomplishments:** Founded the Okapi Conservation Project; director of the White Oak Conservation Center in Yulee, Florida; president of the International Rhino Foundation; cofounder and board member of the Wildlife Conservation Network; past and present board member on various organizations, including Disney's Animal Kingdom, Envirovet, the Cheetah Conservation Fund, the Emerging Wildlife Conservation Leaders, and the Mountain Gorilla Conservation Fund

Okapi

→ **Scientific Name:** *Okapia johnstoni*

→ **Range:** Now limited to forests of the Democratic Republic of the Congo, Africa, okapis are thought to have once been found in Uganda as well.

→ **Population Trend:** Though difficult to assess, the global okapi population is thought to be somewhere between 35,000 and 50,000 individuals, and stable.

→ **IUCN Status:** Near threatened

FORMULATING a conservation strategy for what is possibly the most elusive large mammal on the planet is unquestionably a challenge: how do you save something you can't see, count, or study in its natural habitat? John Lukas has devoted almost a quarter of a century to solving this complex quandary.

"Okapis have evolved to perfectly blend into the forest—I've never actually seen a wild okapi in all my years working to conserve them," says Lukas.

Lukas is the founder of the Okapi Conservation Project (OCP), which he started in 1987. The project operates out of the Epulu Conservation and Research Center located within the Okapi Wildlife Reserve in the Democratic Republic of the Congo (DRC), where as much as one-third of the world's wild okapi population is thought to live. In fact, okapi and leaves are the symbol of all the protected areas of the DRC, reinforcing the link between healthy forests and healthy wildlife populations.

Okapis, readily identified by their dark, velvety coats and black-and-white striped legs and hindquarters, are the only living relative of the giraffe. About the size of a large horse, the okapi was not described by scientists until the start of the twentieth century, long after most other large species had been identified and documented.

The okapi lives exclusively in the Ituri Rainforest of the DRC, considered by many to be the most biologically diverse place in Africa. In addition to

What You Should Know about Okapis

→ Like their only living relative, the giraffe, okapis have unusually long, blue tongues that they use to wrap around branches and pull off leaves.

→ Unlike giraffes, only male okapis have the short, skin-covered hornlike protuberances on their heads, called *ossicones*.

→ The distinctive brown and white markings on the okapi's legs and rear—resembling zebra stripes—help it to blend into the forest.

→ Newborn okapi will stay hidden from predators between six and nine weeks in a "nest" on the forest floor.

Why It Is Important to Save Okapis

The okapi is the flagship species for one of the most biologically diverse spots on Earth—the Democratic Republic of the Congo's Ituri Rainforest. (A flagship species is typically a charismatic, vulnerable animal used to represent an important ecosystem or place in need of public support for conservation).

the shy okapi, Ituri wildlife includes the notoriously amorous bonobo, the Congo peafowl, colobus monkeys, water chevrotains, genets, forest elephants, leopards, and the elegant striped bongo. Within the Ituri Forest, the Okapi Wildlife Reserve occupies almost fourteen thousand square kilometers (nearly eighty-seven hundred square miles) of multiple-use land, still inhabited by local villagers and two tribes of Pygmies.

"Before we came, there were no protected areas for okapi—which was a surprise since they are the national symbol of the country," says Lukas. "We successfully had the Okapi Wildlife Reserve declared in 1992, and worked with the Institute in the Congo for the Conservation of Nature—the government partner charged with managing DRC's protected areas—to develop a management plan to operate the reserve."

When Lukas founded the Okapi Conservation Project, he knew the obstacles that would lie in the way of his efforts. The DRC—called Zaire when the project started—has been in a state of civil unrest and economic crisis throughout much of its history.

"There have been seven occupying armies at the conservation station since I've been involved with okapi conservation," states Lukas. "We've managed to stay relatively safe however, by not taking a political side, and instead always cooperating with the occupiers and keeping close contact with staff in Kinshasa, the capital. Those contacts advise us on security risks and provide guidance on safe passage in and out of the forest, if needed."

When a new occupying force takes over the conservation station, workers aligned with the occupying tribe run the station while those from opposing tribes go into hiding. Then, when the next occupying army comes in, they may have to switch staff entirely to ensure the workers' safety. Despite the many precautions, Lukas and his colleagues at the Reserve are often in danger, and he personally has been shot at in his car and in planes. Relative security has been in place since the end of the war in 2004, as Epulu is quite a distance inland from the troubled eastern border with Uganda and Rwanda.

As difficult a situation as working in the DRC is, the Okapi Conservation Project has incredibly continued almost uninterrupted during the region's regular political upheavals over the past twenty years. Lukas is rightly gratified with that record. "Even while invading armies are wreaking havoc on the forest and killing wildlife for bushmeat, I'm proud to say that no one has ever harmed any of the dozen ambassador okapis that are kept at the center for educational purposes. We've even had local villagers step in to feed those okapis when the Pygmies working at the station were endangered by the occupying army and had to retreat to the forest."

Principle threats to wild okapis include poaching, human encroachment, and loss of habitat. Because of this, the locals will ultimately determine the fate of the species. The assistance of the resident community can be traced to Lukas and his teams' resolute commitment to the people living in and around the reserve. The OCP employs more than two hundred local residents, and many of the initiatives they launch are designed to improve the lives of these people and forest people by providing them secure water sources, accessible health care, and training in sustainable agricultural practices. Additionally, they offer educational opportunities to area children to help them learn about the forest, its wildlife, and sustainable use of natural resources.

One of the OCP's most innovative projects has been introducing alternative protein sources to native residents. As the pressure on okapi and other local wildlife from the bushmeat trade have risen, Lukas and his colleagues have developed a program for new local food sources that have little impact on the surrounding environment. For example, they have supported the experimental Cane Rat Domestication Project, which breeds this indigenous species as a high-protein alternative to bushmeat. Farmers receive assistance with building a breeding facility, some initial breeding stock, and training in how to produce animals for personal consumption and to sell in the markets.

While they are conducting these community outreach programs, Lukas and the OCP staff are also addressing the direct threats to the okapi. This is

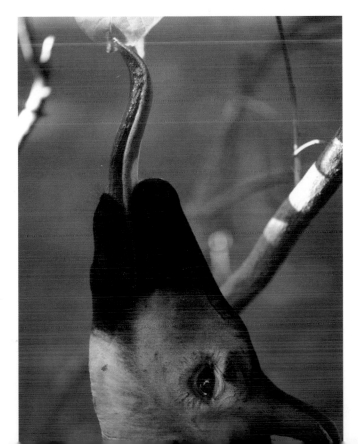

done through training and equipping wildlife guards for the Reserve and supporting their deployment to patrol the forest, where they work to arrest poachers and close down illegal mining and logging operations.

In addition to his impressive okapi conservation efforts, Lukas is an active leader in several other conservation arenas: He is cofounder and board member of the Wildlife Conservation Network, as well as the director of the White Oak Conservation Center in Yulee, Florida. The Center is a world-renowned facility for breeding and research of endangered species, and serves as a training, education, and strategizing epicenter for global leaders in wildlife conservation. As one might imagine, the Center also specializes in studying the biology and reproductive needs of the elusive okapi—using captive breeding to learn more about a species that cannot be studied in the wild. Under Lukas's leadership the Center has developed the most successful captive breeding facility for okapi in the world, and has begun to unravel the mysteries of the mysterious mammal.

"We now know more about the okapi, its biology, and its reliance on the forest than we ever have," says Lukas. "Hopefully this knowledge will help us and those people that share its habitat come up with the right mix of actions to save this incredibly unique species."

LUKE DOLLAR
FOSSA

"My slogan became 'Save the Fossa. Save the Harvest' and it really resonated with locals. All they needed was to make that connection to have a newfound appreciation for the fossa."

Fossa

→ **Scientific Name:** *Cryptoprocta ferox*

→ **Range:** Fossas are only found on the island of Madagascar and require mostly intact forests as their habitat.

→ **Population Trend:** Fossa populations are decreasing as a result of habitat loss and hunting pressures.

→ **IUCN Status:** Vulnerable

Luke Dollar

→ **Education:** PhD from Duke University, North Carolina

→ **Nationality:** American

→ **Organizational Affiliation:** National Geographic; Earthwatch Institute

→ **Years Working with Fossas:** 18

→ **Honors:** Named one of National Geographic's Emerging Explorers (2007)

→ **Notable Accomplishments:** Principal investigator for Earthwatch Institute; first person to capture and study an African wildcat on the island of Madagascar; biology professor at Pfeiffer University in North Carolina

LUKE Dollar was tracking a collared lemur, when he was surprised to come across the shredded remains of the radio collar strewn in with the remnants of the lemur itself. His local guide informed him that the lemur had been attacked and eaten by a mysterious animal called a *fossa*. After Dollar asked around and learned of the fossa's scarcity and persecution by local people, he shifted his research to this animal and committed himself to saving them. In this way, Dollar became the first scientist to launch a major study of the little-known fossa.

By Dollar's best estimate there are fewer than twenty-five hundred fossas left in the wild. The fossa is a medium-sized carnivore once thought to be a member of an ancient cat family, but has since been determined to be a close relative of the mongoose family. A fierce hunter, the fossa has the sleek build of a small feline, the muscled bulk and snout of a canine, the ambling gait of a bear, and the strikingly long tail of a cheetah or puma. It is found only on the African island of Madagascar and is the largest natural predator in the ecosystem. Fossas hunt both during the day and at night and are just as comfortable stalking prey in the treetops as on the ground.

Despite most local people having never actually seen a fossa, Malagasy children grow up hearing stories of their ferocity. Their parents also threaten that if they misbehave, the fossa will come and take them away. As a result, fossas are frequently killed on sight by local farmers and villagers. With this history in mind, Dollar started an education campaign to show the benefits of fossas to farmers. "In addition to lemurs, my research showed that fossas prey on rats and wild pigs—two of the biggest crop-raiding pests Malagasy farmers face," explains Dollar. "My slogan became 'Save the Fossa. Save the Harvest,' and it really resonated with locals. All they needed was to make that connection to have a newfound appreciation for the fossa."

When Dollar saw firsthand how education and outreach can change local attitudes and practices, he expanded his ongoing fossa research and conservation work to include a series of initiatives providing both formal and informal education opportunities to people who live near fossa habitat. With personal funds and money raised from friends and supporters back in the United States, he started a scholarship program for local villagers. The program allowed the first child in a village near his fossa research area to go to secondary school. Since then Dollar's program has sponsored a dozen students, and now for the first time, a child from the village will be attending a university in the fall. The only stipulation Dollar puts on the funding is that sponsored children pledge to go to work in the environmental sector after they finish schooling—as a guide, a ranger, a scientist, or any profession that will benefit the disappearing wildlife of Madagascar.

In Madagascar, Dollar heads up a program for the Earthwatch Institute, where he takes volunteers and scientists into the forests to do research on local carnivores. While fossas are the most notorious carnivores in Madagascar—the fourth largest island in the world—there are other predators as well. In addition to an introduced crocodile species, there are a handful of other carnivores endemic to the island that are as unique as the fossa, including the dark-red ring-tailed mongoose; the small, spotted boky-boky (also known as the *fanaloka* or *striped civet*), and the falanouc, which lives on a diet of worms and stores fat in its tail. These species are typically overshadowed by the fossa in local mythology and international mystique, yet they are perhaps even less known and studied than the fossa. Additionally, Dollar has himself added to the list of carnivores found on Madagascar. He was the first person to capture and study what appears to be an African wildcat—a species suspected to have been introduced to Madagascar hundreds of years ago and until recently, incorrectly thought to be a feral domestic cat sparsely populating the island.

As part of their work, when Dollar and his team of volunteers find a new threat to local carnivores, they also attempt to find answers to solve the problem. For example, in 2003 and 2004, feral dogs moved into the forest where Dollar was working. Immediately, the fossa population went down—possibly due to transference of disease from the dogs, competition for shared resources, or direct predation by the dogs. To counter this, Dollar began a program to eliminate the wild dogs from the forest, and within a year the fossa population in the region resurged to earlier levels.

While Dollar has spent enough time in Madagascar to feel at home there, he has also faced numerous challenges and perils. With little or no modern medical facilities where he works in the field, he has dealt with malaria four times, as well as cholera. He has painfully broken his teeth while eating locally produced rice (the regional processing methods allow for the occasional stone to come through with the rice). He also bears scars from being attacked by a fossa on which he was collecting scientific information (the animal came out of its drugged state sooner than anticipated).

One of Dollar's proudest accomplishments came about in 1999, when he was leading a team of researchers back from the forest and saw a group of local women pounding rice with large pistols; as they crushed the rice, they sang traditional folk songs to the percussive rhythm of the process. Dollar returned later and asked if he could pay them to sing for a group of ecotourists that were visiting the area. He then came back five more times that year with tourist groups, and after each performance began talking with the singers about how they could turn their efforts into income. At the time, the village was completely dependent on slash-and-burn agriculture that was rapidly destroying important fossa habitat. With 90 percent of Madagascar's forests destroyed, habitat loss is the largest threat to the many endemic species of the island.

Inspired by their discussions with Dollar, the women used the money he had been paying them to start a small campground on the site of the former village soccer field. Then Dollar worked with Earthwatch Institute to provide the women's collective with a microloan to expand their campsite. Since then, nearly twenty-five thousand guests have stayed or eaten at the campground. The money from this campsite ecotourism has gotten all the village children into schools and built three wells to provide safe, accessible water. The villagers have also reroofed their houses with permanent materials so they no longer have to regularly take forest wood to refurbish their homes. The ecotourism site provides thirty local people with jobs, and the women who run the campsite still provide regular concerts for their eco-guests.

"Problems and solutions begin and end at the grassroots level," says Dollar, emphatically. "People who live their every minute surrounded by these natural resources make the decisions each day regarding how to use the resources. Providing the right alternatives can tip the scale in favor of sustainable choices." Unfortunately, a new national political party has set back this progress with an aggressive resource exploitation philosophy; however, Dollar is hopeful that the long-term sustainable gains of ecotourism, like that of the women's collective, will come back into favor. And perhaps his education efforts will help make that happen.

"It's a two-pronged approach to conservation. We provide short-term solutions to the adults with an alternative income that decreases their impact on their surroundings. Then we provide a long-term solution to the children by showing them opportunities for education, skills, and awareness beyond the resources of the forest," says Dollar. "The fossa need healthy and happy people in Madagascar; otherwise they will be forced out. No matter how fierce a species it is, it still needs a home to survive. And that's what I'm trying to ensure the fossa has."

What You Should Know about Fossas

→ Fossas are the largest carnivore native to the island of Madagascar.

→ Equally comfortable in trees as on the ground, fossas use their agility and speed to their advantage as expert hunters.

→ Fossas are active both during the day and at night, typically resting during the hottest and coldest periods.

→ Slash-and-burn agriculture, land conversion for crops and pasture, logging, and human expansion have led to significant habitat loss for fossa and other animals found only in Madagascar.

Why It Is Important to Save Fossas

As one of the few predators on Madagascar, fossa help control rats, insects, wild pig and other "pest" populations. They also display unusual behaviors such as female dominance and solitary preference, arboreal hunting, and extremely long mating bouts up in special "mating trees"; many of these distinctive traits have been little studied and could provide valuable evolutionary insights into the unique Madagascar ecosystem.

PATRÍCIA MEDICI
TAPIRS

"Tapirs are not well-known or appreciated for many reasons . . . but studying tapirs in my native country of Brazil is so important because without tapirs, everything in the forest changes."

Tapirs

→ **Species:** There are four species of tapir worldwide.

→ **Range:** The three Western Hemisphere tapirs inhabit wetlands, jungle, and forest in parts of South and Central America, while the Malayan tapir is found in Southeast Asia.

→ **Population Trend:** All tapir species are decreasing in number, with fewer than 3,000 mountain tapirs and 5,500 Baird's tapirs left in the wild.

→ **IUCN Status:** All four species are listed as either Vulnerable or Endangered.

Patrícia Medici

→ **Education:** PhD from Durrell Institute of Conservation and Ecology, University of Kent, United Kingdom

→ **Nationality:** Brazilian

→ **Organizational Affiliation:** Lowland Tapir Conservation Initiative, IPÊ—Instituto de Pesquisas Ecológicas (Institute for Ecological Research), Brazil; IUCN/SSC Tapir Specialist Group

→ **Years Working with Tapirs:** 17

→ **Honors:** Future for Nature Award (2008); Whitley Fund for Nature Award (2008); IUCN Harry Messel Award for Conservation Leadership (2004)

→ **Notable Accomplishments:** IUCN/SSC Tapir Specialist Group chair since 2000; IPÊ (Institute for Ecological Research) founding member; IUCN/SSC Conservation Breeding Specialist Group's Brazil Network facilitator; IUCN/SSC Steering Committee member; coauthored tapir conservation action plans for all four tapir species

STUDYING and conserving the largest land animal in South America—one that, oddly, many people have never even heard of—has been Patrícia Medici's life's work. Medici is a scientist and advocate for the *tapir*—an animal related to rhinos and horses, though it is often incorrectly thought to be quite a few other things—a type of pig because of its shape, an anteater because of its elongated nose, or even a hippo due to its size.

"Tapirs are not well-known or appreciated for many reasons," explains Medici. "It doesn't help that the Portuguese word for *tapir* is *anta*, which can be used to mean 'idiot'—kind of how 'jackass' can be both an animal and a derogatory statement in the English language. But studying tapirs in my native country of Brazil is so important because without tapirs, everything in the forest changes."

Tapirs are large-scale seed dispersers. Considering that a tapir can consume up to eighty-five pounds of fruits, berries, and other vegetation in one day, that's a lot of potential forest regeneration

after seeds are "replanted" in its droppings. In fact, one of Medici's early and still ongoing projects in Brazil's Atlantic Forest region has involved fencing large tracts of forest to prevent tapirs from coming in. The tapirs' absence from these areas soon demonstrates the impact of their loss on forest structure and diversity.

Medici's work in the Atlantic forests of Morro do Diabo State Park also resulted in the capture of thirty-five wild lowland tapirs, twenty-five of which were radio-collared and monitored in the long term. Further, hundreds of biological samples from tapirs were collected and analyzed for genetics and health studies. This was the longest tapir study conducted in Brazil at the time, and it yielded significant amounts of previously unknown biological and ecological information. This data is currently being used to develop recommendations for the conservation of lowland tapirs in the Atlantic Forest biome.

All four species of tapir—three in Latin America and one in Asia—are listed by the IUCN as either Vulnerable or Endangered. Hunting, habitat fragmentation, road kills, and human encroachment into protected areas are prime threats to the tapir's future existence. Medici wants to make sure that the pendulum swings back in their favor, and to do this she knows it takes teamwork. In 2000, Medici became the chair of the IUCN Species Survival Commission Tapir Specialist Group working to save these large, endangered herbivores. Since then, the group has grown to more than 150 committed field researchers, zoo professionals, veterinarians, government agency representatives, conservationists, and students from twenty-seven countries worldwide—all focused on the survival of the four species of tapirs.

"When I first became interested in tapirs and began working in the field, it was an uphill climb to find support," says Medici. "But I soon realized the people who wanted to help were out

What You Should Know about Tapirs

→ Tapirs are strong swimmers, often taking to the water to escape predators.

→ All species of baby tapirs have markings similar to a striped watermelon—this helps them hide on the forest floor.

→ The different tapir species have distinctive traits, such as the black-white-black coloring of the Malay tapir, the woolly coat of the mountain tapir, and the short, stiff mane of the lowland tapir.

→ All species are hunted for food and their tough hides. This combined with habitat loss/fragmentation and road kills are leading factors causing tapir declines.

Why It Is Important to Save Tapirs

Tapirs, known as "gardeners of the forest," are important large seed dispersers, helping to replant the forests in which they live. Because of their size and strength, tapirs also create pathways that other animals use to move through the forests more easily.

them. And we need the people settled in these areas to be involved in protecting tapirs and other wildlife."

IPÊ researchers found that by initiating agroforestry projects with landless families living in tapir and jaguar territory, they could provide both habitat restoration for the wildlife and economic alternatives and income for area residents. The locals are now planting tree species that offer both good cover for wildlife and an eventual harvest for themselves. "The response has been very enthusiastic!" Medici notes. "If people are seeing benefits from their environment, they will be more likely to care for it."

"Through our efforts we have discovered some really interesting things about tapirs: they are not strictly solitary, they are regularly killed and eaten by jaguars and cougars, and they travel a lot within the landscape." But perhaps most important, Medici has found that people who once did not care at all about tapirs will appreciate them if shown why they are such an important and unique forest species.

In 2008, Medici launched the Lowland Tapir Conservation Initiative in Brazil and expanded her tapir conservation efforts to the Brazilian Pantanal. She plans to establish tapir conservation programs in the cerrado and the Amazon Rainforest as well. "By the time I retire from my tapir work, I would like the word *anta* to change in meaning from 'idiot' to something much more appropriate, like 'unique' or 'important,'" she says. "That would be a great accomplishment, and perhaps give tapirs some of the respect they deserve."

there; we just needed to get everyone in contact and working together." That's also the reason Medici and a group of other young biologists, led by Cláudio and Suzana Padua, founded the Brazilian NGO IPÊ—Instituto de Pesquisas Ecológicas (Institute for Ecological Research) in 1991—to bring people together who are interested in conserving Brazil's biodiversity. "Everyone can help. You don't need to be a scientist," says Medici.

Working on solutions to enable tapirs and humans to coexist is another aspect of Medici's work. Through her radio-collaring and tracking research, she has discovered where this large herbivore travels—both inside protected parks and beyond. "Protected areas alone are not large enough to sustain viable populations of tapirs," she warns. "We need both the parks and forest fragments. And corridors through the land connecting

RAOUL DU TOIT
AFRICAN RHINOCEROSES

"When given some space and left to breed without being poached, they are certainly biologically capable of thriving."

African Rhinoceroses

→ **Scientific Name:** Black, *Diceros bicornis*; White, *Ceratotherium simum*

→ **Range:** Southern and eastern Africa

→ **Population Trend:** Large-scale poaching has caused dramatic crashes in populations of both species of African rhinoceroses, and despite some increases in numbers for surviving populations, poaching remains a significant threat.

→ **IUCN Status:** The black rhinoceros is Critically Endangered, and the white rhinoceros is Near Threatened.

Raoul Du Toit

→ **Education:** Master's degree from the University of Cape Town, South Africa

→ **Nationality:** Zimbabwean

→ **Organizational Affiliation:** Lowveld Rhino Trust; International Rhino Foundation

→ **Years Working with Rhinoceros Conservation:** 27

→ **Honors:** Goldman Environmental Prize Award Winner (2011); IUCN Species Survival Commission's Sir Peter Scott Award (2009); WWF Africa and Madagascar Programme Award for Excellence (2003)

→ **Books Published:** *Guidelines for Implementing South African Development Community Rhino Conservation Strategies*

→ **Notable Accomplishments:** Seconded by the Zimbabwean Department of National Parks and Wildlife Management to initiate the Rhino Conservancy Project in Zimbabwe; helped to establish the regional rhino conservation program of the Southern African Development Community; appointed in 1985 to the IUCN African Elephant and Rhino Specialist Group, as scientific officer

DESPITE operating in one of the most politically turbulent and economically challenged countries on Earth, rhino conservationist Raoul du Toit has beaten the odds and managed to increase the rhino populations where he works. For the past twenty-five years, he has been determinedly working to save room for African rhinos in Zimbabwe. "The future of rhinos in my country—in all of Africa, really—will come down to two things: local communities and land use," says du Toit. "How these two interests intersect means everything."

Du Toit was born in Zimbabwe and has lived in southern Africa his entire life. He grew up with wildlife all around him, and built on his developing interest in nature with degrees in zoology and environmental studies. "I never specialized my studies on rhinos, nor did I seek a career in rhino conservation specifically," he says. "I became involved in rhino conservation almost by chance, when I was offered a position with a not-for-profit group that focused on rhino and elephant conservation issues. The real attraction for me, though, was simply the opportunity to visit wild parts of Africa that I had not yet been able to get to. Later, once I was working more directly with rhinos, I became aware that the conservation of these animals is a far more holistic business than I had expected; maintaining the right environment for rhinos to survive really brought me to the leading edge of many conservation and development issues."

Rhinos are relatively modern animals in evolutionary terms, well adapted to a range of habitats, and resistant to livestock-borne diseases from which many other animals in Africa suffer. "When given some space and left to breed without being poached," says du Toit, "they achieve population growth rates of over seven percent per year—so they are certainly biologically capable of thriving."

There are currently five species of rhinoceroses on the planet: the black and white rhinos of Africa; and the Sumatran, Javan, and greater one-horned rhinos of Asia. All the rhinoceros species are in significant crisis, with three (black, Sumatran, and Javan) considered critically endangered, primarily due to aggressive poaching for their horns, which are used in traditional Asian medicines. Poaching, combined with habitat loss, has resulted in the total number of wild rhinos in the world being as low as twenty-five thousand, with

more than two-thirds of those being white rhinos, concentrated in South Africa.

In 1990, with support from WWF and the Beit Trust, du Toit proposed the establishment of the Lowveld Rhino Conservancy Project. The objective was to create a safe area to move black rhinos that would otherwise face extinction due to cross-border poaching on the opposite side of Zimbabwe. This initiative allowed for the conversion of a number of privately owned cattle ranches into wildlife ranches and consolidated them into conservancies large enough in size and sufficiently protected to host viable rhino populations. The initiative grew to be a huge success for the rhinos and other wildlife that returned and prospered within the privately protected areas. The project has been so successful that the Lowveld rhino populations

where du Toit works have increased fivefold, to more than 350 individuals, while rhino populations in other parts of the country continue to decline rapidly from rampant poaching.

In 2009, du Toit converted his project into the Lowveld Rhino Trust, an independent stakeholder-based rhino conservation initiative, becoming its first director. Despite an incredibly difficult job surrounded by political and economic hurdles, du Toit remains idealistic about the rhinos. "There are so many serious problems facing rhino conservation that I devote all my time to creating a livable Africa for the species—luckily I am still fascinated by the rhinos themselves. They are incredibly complex animals in both their behavior and ecology. The continuing inspiration I get from wild rhinos keeps me going in this job every day."

Rhinoceroses are all plant-eaters, with thick skin and either one or two horns on their upper snouts. The horns are made of compressed keratin, the same protein material that makes up human fingernails and hair. Rhinos are related to horses, zebras, and tapirs, and their shaggy ancestor—the woolly rhino—may have existed in Europe and Asia as recently as ten thousand years ago. Prehistoric cave paintings of humans hunting woolly rhinos may give a clue to the cause of their extinction. The Sumatran rhino is the last representative of the woolly rhinoceros family; however, like all the rhino species, and most other remaining megafauna species (like elephants, bears, and whales), they continue to struggle with human-caused threats to their continued existence.

While du Toit has had significant successes in his work with black and white rhinos, challenges of a recent chaotic land-reform movement in Zimbabwe have left du Toit and his colleagues struggling to adapt and secure new, meaningful incentives for local people to keep rhinos on private lands. "Zimbabwe had a vibrant private-sector wildlife industry when we started our efforts in the '80s—the burden of rhino protection was spread onto the private sector, who were also able to benefit from ecotourism from rhinos

What You Should Know about Rhinoceroses

→ The closest living relatives to rhinos are tapirs and horses.

→ Rhinos once spread across North America, Europe, Africa, and Asia, and occupied diverse ecosystems, including tropical, temperate, and even Arctic habitats.

→ The Southern white rhinoceros is the most numerous of all surviving rhino subspecies, however the Northern white rhinoceros subspecies is presumed to be extinct in the wild.

→ There are three species of Asian rhino: the Sumatran rhino and the Javan rhino, both of which are Critically Endangered, and the Indian rhino, which is considered Vulnerable to extinction.

→ The Sumatran rhino retains some of the long, shaggy hair characteristic of its relative the woolly rhino, which went extinct about ten thousand years ago.

and other wildlife. Since then, however, live rhinos have lost their commercial value under current policies—tourism has collapsed, and poaching has increased. We need to find a way to rebuild economic rhino value for communities in order to save rhinos here right now, and also in the long run."

With these new hurdles in mind, du Toit and the Lowveld Rhino Trust have developed a unique rhino conservation scheme directly linking conservation success to an unexpected community benefit: support for Zimbabwe's rural community schools. "Traditional foreign aid from other governments and not-for-profit organizations has caused jealousy, nepotism, and political manipulation. Schools are different—they are seen as a community service providing benefits to all members of the community." The Trust is proposing that successful security and breeding of endangered rhinos are directly rewarded with support for community schools adjacent to wildlife conservancies. For relatively little money, organizations and individuals concerned with saving the rhino can help the Trust provide basic teaching materials, scholarships, and other tools to improve rural education. In exchange, native residents who are best situated to ensure the rhinos' survival will be expected to protect them. "In Zimbabwe, poachers typically come from outside the community, so if the local people know that safe and happy rhinos mean better schools, they will block outsiders from coming and killing their rhinos."

"Our experience in Zimbabwe—where we have far less resources to tackle rhino poaching than many other range countries—shows that steady effort in exposing crime syndicates, translocating rhinos out of unsecure areas, along with other strategic interventions, can bring poaching under control," says du Toit. "But it will always come down to the local people and how they value their wildlife. Rhinos-for-schools is just one way to make this connection."

LEANDRO SILVEIRA
JAGUAR

"It will not be easy to save the species because jaguars and humans are competing for the same resources, but we've already made progress, and we will continue to make more. Our passion for this animal keeps us going."

Jaguar

→ **Scientific Name:** *Panthera onca*

→ **Range:** The jaguar's geographic range extends from the Southwest United States to lower Argentina, with nearly 50 percent of its distribution in Brazil.

→ **Population Trend:** Although the population is globally declining, jaguars can still be found in nineteen countries in the Western Hemisphere.

→ **IUCN Status:** Near Threatened

Leandro Silveira

→ **Education:** PhD in animal biology from the University of Brasília, Brazil

→ **Nationality:** Brazilian

→ **Organizational Affiliation:** Jaguar Conservation Fund

→ **Years Working with Jaguars:** 20+

→ **Notable Accomplishments:** Founded the Jaguar Conservation Fund; principal investigator for the Earthwatch Institute; working to explore and protect the 2,000-mile Brazilian Araguaia River as a jaguar conservation corridor connecting the Amazon jungle and cerrado grassland ecosystems

LEANDRO Silveira knows that the best way to save jaguars is to get all levels of Brazilian society on his side. "Everyone is always interested in getting the governor or environmental ministers on board with conservation," he says. "While these are important players whom we work with regularly at the Jaguar Conservation Fund, it is the people living alongside jaguars who will ultimately determine the fate of the species."

This is why Silveira's organization has focused for years on educating local people and showing them the benefits of conserving jaguars. Over a decade ago he started the Annual Jaguar Festival in the Pantanal—the Brazilian wetlands, where the healthiest population of jaguars in South America is thought to live. Once a year, Silveira's organization would bring in free medical and dental care for the locals, along with fun activities for families and educational presentations about jaguars and their importance for the biological and economic security of the region. "We continue to work with the landowners, compensating them when there are confirmed kills of cattle by jaguars, but in the end, it is the ranch hands and locals who actually hunt the jaguars that are considered a 'problem'; so it is vital that we reach these people as well as the politicians and landowners."

Silveira, who is known for his deadpan sense of humor and pranks on unsuspecting visitors to his field stations, is always serious when working with wild jaguars. "One time we were tracking a jaguar in the Pantanal Amazon, when one of the locals decided to show off to our team for a camera crew. He ran up on a cornered adult female jaguar, who

What You Should Know about Jaguars

→ The jaguar is exclusively carnivorous, with more than 85 identified species in its diet.

→ Adult jaguars are solitary, primarily only interacting with other jaguars during mating periods.

→ Unusual among felines, jaguars are comfortable in the water and are strong swimmers.

→ Jaguars use roaring, scat, urine marking, and scratching of trees as methods of communication.

→ A small percentage of jaguars are melanistic, with black fur that makes their spot pattern difficult to see. Although these cats are often referred to as "black panthers," they are still members of the jaguar species.

Why It Is Important to Save Jaguars

At the top of the food chain in Central and South America, jaguars are vital for controlling populations of midlevel predators. In the absence of top-level predators, the health of an ecosystem can decline rapidly.

of course jumped at him. Our team members had to run forward and help pull the jaguar off the man's arm, and now he and one of my colleagues have the scars to show for it."

As the largest predator in the Western Hemisphere, the jaguar boasts a range that stretches from southern Arizona to northern Argentina. Its presence is vital for the equilibrium of the ecosystems in which it lives, as it helps maintain healthy levels of prey species, such as peccaries, deer, and tapirs. Jaguar habitat is diminishing rapidly due to agricultural expansion and development—the species has already been eliminated from many parts of its range. In Brazil, the jaguar's original distribution range has decreased by 48 percent, and less than 6 percent of its habitat is protected from future development.

Although many people admire the species as a symbol of power and beauty, farmers lose cattle to them annually and view them as dangerous pests. Most farmers are also terrified that they will themselves be killed and eaten by jaguars; therefore, convincing them to protect the species on their land is extremely difficult. This is a deep-rooted attitude, forged by centuries of conflict and fear.

After years of conducting jaguar research and starting conservation efforts in the Pantanal, Silveira founded the Jaguar Conservation Fund in 2002 with his wife, fellow wildlife biologist Anah Jácomo. Through Silveira and Jácomo's work and educational efforts in the Pantanal, the jaguar is now flourishing in the region, and native residents have a new appreciation for jaguars and their historical, cultural, and economic role in the area.

Silveira has led significant scientific research on jaguars, not only in the Pantanal, but also in the five other biomes of Brazil that still hold viable jaguar populations. And his latest, most ambitious project has been mapping and researching a twenty-one-hundred-mile stretch of river connecting the Brazilian Pantanal and grasslands (or *cerrado*) to the Amazon basin. "This amazing and mostly undisturbed habitat is not only a vital

wildlife corridor for jaguars who use the riparian zone for hunting, shelter, and seeking mates," he explains, "but also for other key species, such as pink river dolphins, lowland tapirs, giant river otters, and giant catfish." Silveira hopes to generate enough scientific data to give the Brazilian government everything they need to declare the entire stretch of the Araguaia River a conservation corridor—complete with legal protections and monitoring to ensure that it remains a wildlife highway free from threats to jaguars and other important Brazilian species.

Since the age of fourteen, Silveira has known that his life would be devoted to jaguar conservation. He has continued his conservation work while facing physical danger, confronting cultural hurdles, and challenging institutionalized prejudices in his native country of Brazil—all in the hope of saving this great cat in his own homeland and throughout its range. "The impressive beauty of the jaguar," says Silveira, "has instilled a passion in both myself and my wife, Anah, and hopefully one day our son, Tiago, too. It will not be easy to save the species because jaguars and humans are competing for the same resources, but we've already made progress, and we will continue to make more. Our passion for this animal keeps us going."

ELENA BYKOVA
SAIGA

"With the saiga we've witnessed the fastest decline of any mammal species on Earth in just over one decade."

Saiga

→ **Scientific Name:** *Saiga tatarica*

→ **Range:** Found in steppes and semi desert of Southeastern Europe and Central Asia; extinct in China since the 1960s.

→ **Population Trend:** In 1975 there were 1,250,000 individuals, but in 2010, there were only between 90,000 and 100,000 individuals.

→ **IUCN Status:** Critically Endangered

Elena Bykova

→ **Education:** Master's degree from Tyumen State University, Russia

→ **Nationality:** Uzbek

→ **Organizational Affiliation:** Saiga Conservation Alliance

→ **Years Working with Saigas:** 8

→ **Honors:** Whitley Award recipient (2011); Marsh Foundation Award (2009)

→ **Notable Accomplishments:** Founding member and trustee for the Saiga Conservation Alliance; Wildlife Conservation Network partner

SCIENTISTS Elena Bykova and her husband, Alexander Esipov, visited the Ustyurt plateau in remote Uzbekistan in 2004 to conduct research on the herds of saiga antelope that they had seen congregate there by the thousands just six years earlier. Instead, they found the landscape filled with only skulls and skeletons. These grisly remains were saiga carcasses—most likely left behind by poachers who took the meat and removed the valuable horns, leaving the animals' remains to decompose on the boundless desert plain.

The saiga antelope is one species rarely heard about unless you happen to be from where they are found, which Bykova is. A native of Uzbekistan, she finds these animals irresistible. "Saigas are a unique species with strange adaptations. Just its nose alone makes it weird—but there's a reason for it. In summer, the large nose acts like a giant filter to keep out sand and dust. And in winter, it warms the air on the way to the lungs."

Saigas are ancient animals, having lived on the planet at the same time as the mammoths and saber-toothed cats more than sixty thousand years ago. They are a keystone species for the areas they inhabit; many other native creatures cannot digest the coarse plants on which the saiga thrives. Thus, these animals are instrumental in the shaping of the vegetation in their ecosystem, creating ecological niches for the other species that share the region. Wolves, birds of prey, foxes, ground nesting birds, and even rodents are all dependent on the saiga to provide access to grazed vegetation. "Without the saiga, we lose it all," points out Bykova.

Saigas, however, are in real danger of disappearing from the Earth. Not only are the animals hunted for meat, but the male's horns are highly sought after by poachers for use in traditional Chinese medicines. Poaching for horn is so widespread that few mature males remain, setting up fierce competition among females, leaving many unbred and further diminishing the populations. The situation has been exacerbated by the hardship and poverty resulting from the breakup of the former Soviet Union. Full-scale poaching has led to an almost unbelievable 95 percent decline of saigas in less than two decades. Paradoxically, it was Russia's strength that saved saigas from disappearing in the early 1900s. Even then horns were prized, but laws and enforcement allowed herds to grow. Saiga antelopes used to be so numerous they were routinely hunted and traded across the steppes of Asia and Russia without a second thought. Now, with unchecked poaching, there are thought to be fewer than one hundred thousand left.

"I went to the Ustyurt plateau naively as a scientist going to study the reproductive biology of an interesting animal in the wild," relates Bykova. "I left the area knowing I also needed to be a conservationist working to save a wonderfully unique species from being totally wiped out."

In 2006, Elena joined a handful of other saiga specialists to form the Saiga Conservation Alliance, a group dedicated to working throughout the saiga's range to draw attention to its plight. Through the Saiga Conservation Alliance, or SCA, Bykova has striven to get local communities within the species' range involved in saiga protection rather than persecution. Developing alternative incomes to poaching, spearheading educational programs for children, monitoring and protecting populations, and advocating for government support are all part of SCA's goals and activities. "Partnerships and collaboration are a big part of preserving species, so besides my field research," states Bykova, "I've focused much of my efforts into bringing people together." A unique bulletin, the

What You Should Know about Saigas

→ Saigas once roamed the Eurasian plains at the same time as woolly rhinoceroses and mammoths.

→ There was a 95 percent decline in the saiga population just between 1995 and 2009.

→ A saiga's large nose acts to warm incoming air in the winter and filter out dust in the summer.

→ Saigas can recover with protection. Their populations can increase by an astounding 60 percent in just one year under optimal conditions.

Why It Is Important to Save Saigas

Saigas are instrumental in shaping the vegetation in their ecosystem, creating ecological niches for other species that share the region, such as wolves, foxes, and nesting birds.

Saiga News, printed in six languages, including Russian, Mongolian, Chinese, Kazakh, and Uzbek, has helped bring all those concerned about the future of saigas together and kept them informed about the latest species and conservation news.

But Elena feels that her most important success is reaching the local people and teaching about what's happening to their native wildlife. "Many people didn't believe they should think about the saiga if their families haven't enough food," states Bykova. "But what the locals didn't realize was how current trends are unsustainable, and what was happening had already happened once before." In fact, older people from the Ustyurt villages remembered when the saigas first returned to the plateau after having been extirpated from the area, and tell of an ancient legend. Bykova recounts the tale: "Saiga will rescue you and your family—it will feed you and show you the best pastures and watering places. But you should not kill the saiga for profit, because it is your brother." Through education, research, employment and volunteer opportunities, and celebration of this important animal, the saiga is gaining support—even from those who used to poach. "I can't say that 100 percent of the Ustyurt population has stopped hunting and begun to act for conservation, but their vision has started to change. People are now more likely to want to save saigas for their children—to have the steppe alive with saigas, rather than a dead steppe without them."

CLAUDIA FEH
PRZEWALSKI'S HORSE

"For this to work, we need to give the horses all the best conditions that they can have to survive in the wild . . . Then we need to wait."

Przewalski's Horse

→ **Scientific Name:** *Equus ferus przewalskii*

→ **Range:** Once found across Eurasia from eastern Europe to Russia, and in Mongolia and China, they are now extinct in the wild, with various reintroduction projects under way in Mongolia and China.

→ **Population Trend:** Captive populations and reintroduced wild populations are increasing.

→ **IUCN Status:** Critically Endangered

Claudia Feh

→ **Education:** University thesis at Université d'Aix–Marseille II, Faculté des Sciences de Luminy, France

→ **Nationality:** Swiss

→ **Organizational Affiliation:** Association pour le Cheval de Przewalski: Takh (the Association for the Przewalski's Horse)

→ **Years Working with Przewalski's Horses:** 30

→ **Honors:** Rolex Award for Enterprise (2004)

→ **Notable Accomplishments:** Created the Association for the Przewalski's Horse (Takh); reintroduced a new population of Przewalski's horses back into Mongolia.

AT a time when wildlife news is overwhelmingly dire, with species after species continuing to move closer to extinction, Claudia Feh is taking steps to do something many people think impossible: bring a species back. Feh is working to reintroduce the Przewalski's horse back to the wild after nearly half a century's absence.

The Przewalski's horse—also known as the Asian wild horse, or *takhi*—was last seen in the wilds of Mongolia in the late 1960s. The species is closely related to the domestic horse and other equids, such as zebras and wild asses. Wild horses, of which the Przewalski's horse is a subspecies, were previously found across Eurasia from eastern Europe to Russia and down through Mongolia and China. They suffered a steep decline in the 1800s,

and the Przewalski's horse is the last living specimen from the species. A number of factors are believed to have contributed to the decline of wild horses, including hunting, competition with livestock, habitat loss to human encroachment and agricultural conversion, and climactic change. Additionally, a series of abnormally harsh winters between 1945 and 1956, and capture expeditions for scientific and private collections, are thought to have hastened the disappearance of Przewalski's horses from Asia.

Feh was only fifteen years old when the last Przewalski's horse was spotted in the wild. At that time she was already creating a bond with equids through riding domesticated horses. Horseback riding gave her the opportunity to explore the

Why It Is Important to Save Przewalski's Horses

The Przewalski's horse represents the wild horse family that has gone extinct with the exception of this sub-species, kept alive through a small, captive population. A successful reintroduction into the wild could provide lessons for reintroductions of other large grazers that have entirely disappeared from the wild, like Père David's deer and the scimi-tar-horned oryx.

What You Should Know about Wild Horses

→ There are seven surviving species of wild equids: three of zebras (Grevy's, plains, and mountain), three of wild asses (Asiatic, African, and kiang), and one of wild horses (Przewalski's).

→ Cave paintings and engravings in Europe that resemble Przewalski's horses in color and shape indicate that there may have been wild horses in western Europe thirty thousand years ago.

→ All Przewalski's horses alive today are descendents of fewer than fifteen individuals, most of which were captured from the wild at the turn of the nineteenth century.

→ Przewalski's horses typically have short, erect manes, tails with short bristle hairs, and some dark striping seen on the mane, back, tail, and legs.

→ Wild horses are genetically very similar to domestic horses.

Swiss countryside, and as a result, her appreciation of equids and wild landscapes evolved together. Her first real studies of the horse family also started early on. "It began in secondary school," she recalls, "where I was motivated by a particularly inspiring biology teacher to do an independent project researching zebras at the Zurich zoo. That study of captive zebras was my first window into the 'wild' equid world. After I finished school, I spent eight years gathering data on a group of mostly free-roaming domesticated horses in Southern France, where I logged seven thousand hours of observation."

"Wild" horse populations found today in parts of Europe, Australia, India, and North America are in fact feral domesticated horses, not true wild horses, like Przewalski's horses. Although genetically very similar, Przewalski's horses have a number of physical and biological traits that differ from domestic horses. For example, they typically have short, erect manes and short bristle hairs on their tails that they shed annually, unlike domestic horses, which tend to have flowing manes and tails that they retain year-round.

While studying domestic horses, Feh learned that the last true wild horses—Przewalski's horses—had been declared extinct in the wild in the late 1960s. The individual survivors left in captivity all descended from fewer than fifteen horses saved in a captive breeding operation, their descendants now mostly scattered in zoos in Europe and North America. "These remaining animals lived in small areas and had limited opportunity to live the normal socially rich life of a wild equid," Feh says. "After studying free-ranging horses for so many years, I knew how important social behavior was for the survival of horses, and their current situations did not do them justice. I decided I had to do something about it."

Feh connected with acclaimed conservationist Luc Hoffman, who was willing to support her idea of creating a socially

natural herd of Przewalski's horses. She then acquired enough individuals from existing captive collections to start a relatively unmanaged population near the village of Le Villaret in southeast France. At the time, Feh's main motivation was not to breed for reintroduction, but instead to create a setting that would allow Przewalski's horses to interact as they might in the wild. She was successful and is credited with starting the first natural herd, which lived and bred in the Le Villaret countryside for ten years with nearly no intervention by Feh or her coworkers. At this point, Feh was ready to launch the reintroduction plans that she had been forming for the last few years of the project.

"There were already two different reintroduction efforts started in Mongolia by European not-for-profit groups," she explains. "We brought twenty-two horses over to a site in western Mongolia between 2004 and 2005, and have practiced only limited intervention since then—although we do provide emergency care when necessary. With less than two thousand total Przewalski's horses left in the world, we cannot afford to needlessly lose even one. And we have been very lucky in that we have only lost a small number of our horses as part of this

reintroduction effort. As a matter of fact, the horses have successfully reared half a dozen foals that are now part of the herd. But a successful reintroduction is defined by a free viable population, and we have a long way to go to achieve that. This doesn't mean we aren't doing well in our efforts. Horses are big animals with low reproductive output. They typically foal every other year, making for an extremely fragile population. These projects will take a long time."

Simultaneously, China—another historic range country for Przewalski's horse—is engaged in a number of projects looking to "rewild" formerly captive-bred Przewalski's horses. However, those populations are still kept in barns half of the year to ensure that the horses are able to survive the harshest months, so they have not yet had to withstand the true test of a wild existence.

Feh's reintroduction effort in Seeriin Nuruu, in western Mongolia, is situated on a fourteen-thousand-hectare site (about thirty-five thousand acres) enclosed by a river, a mountain, and a fence built to keep domestic animals out and protect the habitat from overgrazing. The horses occasionally leave the site to visit a local lake, but mostly stay in the relatively protected site. The Seeriin Nuruu project horses, as well as all the reintroduced populations, face multiple modern threats, but chief among them is the threat of hybridization and disease transmission from domestic horses. Because of this, much of Feh's efforts include reaching out to, and incorporating, local people in the initiative—ensuring that they are an integral part of the project. "For this to work," she says, "we need to give the horses all the best conditions that they can have to survive in the wild: support from nomadic herders that share the ecosystem; multiple, simultaneous reintroduction efforts to provide safety nets and genetic diversity; safe environments to begin the re-acclimation process. Then we need to wait." And Feh is willing to take the time to make sure it is done right.

In 2004, Feh's tremendous efforts were recognized when she was awarded the prestigious Rolex Award for Enterprise. "Dedicating my life to working with wild horses has been wonderful. It is not a sacrifice, but an honor. We are in an extinction crisis. There are over one thousand mammal species listed as imperiled on the IUCN Red List of threatened species. Something has to be done to stop this loss. I am making my contribution to helping life survive on this planet. Bringing those first twenty-two horses back to Mongolia was my start."

EUGENE RUTAGARAMA
MOUNTAIN GORILLA

"The gorillas represented something of value that could help my fellow Rwandans heal. The mountain gorillas are a national treasure—we recognize they must be protected—especially during the most difficult times."

Mountain Gorilla

→ **Scientific Name:** *Gorilla gorilla beringei*

→ **Range:** All mountain gorillas live within three countries, split between two mountainous regions: the Virunga Volcanoes of Rwanda, Democratic Republic of the Congo and Uganda, and Bwindi Impenetrable National Park in Uganda.

→ **Population Trend:** Officially unknown, although populations appear to be slowly increasing. There are fewer than 800 mountain gorillas left in the world.

→ **IUCN Status:** Critically Endangered

Eugene Rutagarama

→ **Education:** Master's of science from the University of East Anglia, United Kingdom

→ **Nationality:** Rwandan

→ **Organizational Affiliation:** International Gorilla Conservation Program

→ **Years Working with Mountain Gorillas:** 16

→ **Honors:** Featured as a "Defending the Planet" CNN Hero (2007); Charlotte Conservation Fellowship (2002); the Goldman Environmental Prize, conservation's equivalent to the Nobel Prize (2001); the Getty Prize for Wildlife Conservation (1996)

→ **Books Published:** *Le Regard du Gorille*

→ **Notable Accomplishments:** Returned to Rwanda after the genocide to accept the position of deputy director of the national parks system, returning order, operations, and protection for the gorillas of Rwanda; the first African director of the International Gorilla Conservation Program

IT'S hard to imagine a more dangerous time and place than Rwanda in the early 1990s. The human persecution, suffering, and death toll both before and during the genocide were immeasurable. Like so many of his fellow Rwandans, Eugene Rutagarama was forced to leave the country, but his empathy for both the humans who remained and the vulnerable gorillas who represented such a unique aspect of Rwandan fauna, propelled him to return. "The gorillas represented something of value that could help my fellow Rwandans heal," he said. "The mountain gorillas are a national treasure—we recognize they must be protected—especially during the most difficult times."

Before the civil war began, Rutagarama was studying the regeneration of trees in Volcanoes National Park, one of the few areas in Africa where mountain gorillas survive. Upon his return, he had a mission—to make sure nothing happened to the gorillas he had come to know and love. Rutagarama

What You Should Know about Gorillas

→ Gorillas are primarily herbivorous, eating up to 45 pounds daily of more than 100 different varieties of plants, roots, shoots, leaves, bark, flowers, and fruit.

→ Gorillas are not aggressive animals, but will pound their chests, vocalize, throw vegetation, and display other behaviors to assert dominance without actually fighting.

→ The main threats to the mountain gorilla are being caught in snares or traps often set for other animals, habitat loss, and poaching, often linked to political unrest in the region.

→ Mountain gorillas have very little habitat left, having been restricted to the highest altitudes of mountainous areas. Worse, there is pressure to convert even this land to agriculture to help feed growing human populations.

→ The leader of each family group, known as the *silverback*, will defend the group to his death.

signed on as deputy director of the Rwandan Wildlife Service—a government agency in disarray and undermanned, as many park staff had been killed or had fled. Additionally, the national parks were under tremendous pressure to be cultivated and converted to living space for the hundreds of thousands of refugees beginning to return with no place to go in such a small country. The parks were a natural target for much-needed resettlement space. As a result, Rutagarama entered into the job with his own battle to fight: to help the people, while also preserving enough land for the wildlife of Rwanda—especially the critically endangered mountain gorillas.

There are just 790 mountain gorillas left in the wild today, found in only three Central African countries—Rwanda, Uganda, and Democratic Republic of the Congo. Mountain gorillas can live at higher, colder altitudes than their lowland cousins due to their longer, thicker hair and slightly larger size, reaching five hundred pounds and over six feet tall. Males attain their characteristic gray or silver hair when they mature, at about thirteen to fifteen years of age. Mountain gorillas live in troops, with both males and females eventually leaving the group into which they were born, to begin new families. These related groups often peacefully share their lush mountain habitat. A successful silverback—or dominant male—may have anywhere from two to ten adult females and associated offspring in his family—which he will protect with his life.

"Gorillas are amazing animals. As a species, they are mostly easygoing, gentle animals. Males are so tolerant of the little ones who sometimes climb all over them while they are trying to eat or rest. And yet they are firm leaders as well, deciding when to move, where to go, and being watchful for danger the entire time."

Preserving resources and protecting this extraordinary species have become Rutagarama's life passion. Despite overwhelming humanitarian demands in his country, he successfully

Why It Is Important to Save Mountain Gorillas

Due to the large quantities of plant matter they consume, gorillas play an important role in the shaping of plant and forest environments. Tourism to view gorillas in their wild habitat is an important part of the range country economies, bringing millions of dollars each year into Rwanda, Uganda, and Democratic Republic of the Congo.

convinced the Rwandan government of the need to conserve the remaining gorilla habitat and even received the aid of Rwandese Patriotic Army soldiers to whom he had foresightedly helped provide training, to prevent incursions of displaced people into park boundaries. Once the boundaries were firmly established, he then set about restructuring, recruiting, and re-staffing the entire wildlife service. "If we can save our gorillas, we can lay a real foundation for a sustainable and healthy tourism industry based on gorilla viewing. If we can do this," Rutagarama maintains, "then the entire country will benefit. But that will only happen if we set aside a safe place for the gorillas to live and thrive right now."

Rutagarama received two prestigious awards: the Getty Prize for Wildlife Conservation in 1996 and the Goldman Environmental Prize—equivalent to the Nobel Prize, but in the area of conservation—in 2001, for his efforts, in which he often risked his life and thus had saved those of the mountain gorillas. "I finally felt we had a structure and plan within Rwanda, which was fantastic," he said. "But it wasn't enough. All three range countries are essential to the survival of this great ape. And I wanted to be more involved at that level."

Earlier in his career, Rutagarama had worked as a program officer in Rwanda, in an organization called the International Gorilla Conservation Programme (IGCP), formed and supported by three organizations—the African Wildlife Foundation, Flora & Fauna International, and the World

Wildlife Fund. After Rutagarama's experience with the Rwandan government, he assumed control of IGCP as director in 2003. Later, he won a coveted spot among CNN's Heroes for "Defending the Planet."

Since making his career change, Rutagarama has continued to have his work cut out for him. Rwanda is one of the most densely populated countries in the world, with more than 85 percent of its people depending on subsistence farming and agriculture. Fertile soil has supported such a large population, but that only creates a worsening problem—the need for more land to support the expanding requirements for resources. "IGCP works with all three range state governments, committed NGOs, and most importantly, the local communities, to ensure all are involved and benefiting from the presence of gorillas. It's the only way it's going to work."

And it has been working. One of the few critically endangered species that has actually increased in number over the past twenty years, the mountain gorilla has become the poster child for successful conservation, under Rutagarama's guidance. With a multipronged approach including antipoaching patrols, group monitoring, community development projects, habitat protection, and education, Rutagarama is helping the gorillas make a comeback. "We've been through a lot, these gorillas and us Rwandans," he says. "We are all moving forward with increased optimism for a more positive future; recovering together, sharing the land and future with the mountain gorillas."

SHIVANI BHALLA
LION

"My dream to devote my life to saving a
species has pretty much come true.
Knowing lions are in such rapid decline has
made my work and my mission even
more meaningful."

FAST FACTS

Lion

→ **Scientific Name:** *Panthera leo*

→ **Range:** While lions were historically found in eastern Europe, Asia, and across Africa, today they are only found in sub-Saharan Africa, and in one small, isolated population in India.

→ **Population Trend:** Declining in number, lion populations have dropped 30 percent in the past two decades. There are suspected to be fewer than 40,000 left in the wild today.

→ **IUCN Status:** Vulnerable

Shivani Bhalla

→ **Education:** Master's degree from Edinburgh Napier University, United Kingdom

→ **Nationality:** Kenyan

→ **Organizational Affiliation:** Ewaso Lion Project

→ **Years Working with Lions:** 9

→ **Honors:** Received "Africa's Young Women Conservation Biologist" of the year award from the Society of Conservation Biology (2009)

→ **Books:** Editor of *Simba Stories*, a collection of stories and drawings about lions by students in Samburu, Kenya

→ **Notable Accomplishments:** Founded the Ewaso Lion Project; Emerging Wildlife Conservation Leaders graduate; Bronze-level guide with the Kenya Professional Safari Guides Association

SHIVANI Bhalla is fulfilling her dream by helping a species survive. "As a child," she says, "I read about Dian Fossey, who worked tirelessly to conserve mountain gorillas, and about Joy and George Adamson, whom the movie *Born Free* was based on. I wanted to do what they did—live in the wild, drive around, look for animals, and work to save them."

As Bhalla was born and raised in Kenya, it was natural for her parents to introduce her to wildlife early in life. She began her career path by working for the Kenya Wildlife Service, then as a guide in Samburu, Kenya. Being hired as an education officer for Save the Elephants, a well-established Samburu research organization, gave her the opportunity to acquaint herself with the local communities and discover how much she actually enjoyed working with people and teaching youth about conservation. From this job, a PhD and a long-term project to help people and lions eventually evolved into the Ewaso Lion Project—an organization she founded. There is little known of the lion populations in the Ewaso Nyiro region, which includes three national reserves and a large community conservancy in northern Kenya. Bhalla is working to address not only the knowledge gap, but attitudes about lions in general.

The Ewaso Nyiro ecosystem where Bhalla works is an arid, remote environment with an increasingly large population of people and livestock, who, along with wildlife, are all trying to survive on minimal resources. Conflict between powerful predators, especially the social, very visible lions and local residents, is growing. Humans are causing much of the lions' decline, mostly due to fragmentation through habitat occupation and shooting and poisoning in retaliation for loss of cattle to predation. "Lions' historic range and numbers have been so drastically reduced, I'm just trying to keep them from being exterminated in northern Kenya and make people more aware we're losing this iconic predator all across Africa," states Bhalla.

Much of Bhalla's efforts include working with the local people to help them understand that lions are an important apex predator whose loss will change the ecosystem in many, as yet undetermined, ways. Some scientists estimate that lion numbers have dropped as much as 30 to 40 percent over the last two decades alone. In the 1950s the number of lions in Africa was estimated at about four hundred thousand. Today, there are

What You Should Know about Lions

→ Lions are one of the four "great cats"—another name for the big cats that roar: lions, jaguars, tigers, and leopards.

→ Lions, being the most social of the big cats, form prides typically made up of related females, their dependent young, and one or more immigrant males.

→ Threats to African lions include killings in retaliation for human-lion conflict, loss of habitat and prey base, disease, and overexploitation from trophy hunting and commercial trade in lion parts.

→ A loss of a dominant male in a pride can render the pride vulnerable to takeover by outside males, thereby allowing for add-on deaths from a power struggle, and potential infanticides if the pride is successfully taken over.

→ The subspecies of Asiatic lions is considered Endangered, with only a few hundred individuals surviving.

thought to be fewer than forty thousand. But since these prolific felines can have large litters, Bhalla believes lions have the ability to rebound if just given protection, space, and the prey resources they need. "The hard part is surviving," she says. "Between avoiding humans, finding enough prey, keeping your territory, and staying healthy and injury free, being a successful lion is no easy task. But they were doing well for centuries—it's not until relatively recently that numbers have fallen so drastically. But I think with knowledge and education, we can turn this around."

In the beginning Bhalla knew little about her subject and could not tell one lion in the field from another. Now, she's not only able to recognize individual lions from afar and knows what areas each

lion prefers when in Samburu, but she also knows the pride structures, when conflicts with locals occur, and many of the threats to the lions' survival. After spending so much time with lions, one would think she'd take seeing them in stride. But no, Bhalla says. "Each time I see them is thrilling for me, as if each time is the first time I've ever seen lions in the wild."

In order to conduct her work, Shivani lives most of the year in an eight-by-seven-foot tent, with no electricity or running water—or protection from wild neighbors. "Visitors to the camp are surprised when they see we are in the middle of nowhere. We regularly hear hyenas or other unseen animals sniffing around the tents, or elephants knocking down trees at night."

The location is so remote, inhospitable, and at times, insecure, there are few opportunities to socialize outside of the local populations. But this makes for stronger bonds—and opportunities for information exchange. To effectively communicate with as many people as possible, Bhalla has learned many languages—Swahili, French, Hindi, English, and Samburu. She has earned the trust and respect of the people among whom she lives and works. "I care about the local Samburu people, and they care about me—there is a trust factor," she says. "It has not been easy, but I feel like I am making a difference. My dream to devote my life to saving a species has pretty much come true. Knowing lions are in such rapid decline has made my work and my mission even more meaningful."

Why Is It Important to Save Lions

"The King of the Jungle" has been an icon in mythology, history and culture around the world for thousands of years and is used to symbolize bravery, strength and leadership. In its natural habitat, it sits at the top of the food chain with only man, and Nile crocodiles in the water, daring to attack healthy adult lions.

CLAUDIO SILLERO
ETHIOPIAN WOLF

"If we can shift our efforts from reacting to threats, to instead proactively managing them—like providing vaccinations before a disease outbreak—Ethiopian wolves will be able to survive into the future."

FAST FACTS

Ethiopian Wolf

→ **Scientific Name:** *Canis simensis*

→ **Range:** Seven isolated populations in mountain enclaves of the Ethiopian highlands

→ **Population Trend:** Disease outbreaks in 1991, 2003, and 2008 caused dramatic declines in key populations. There are currently only 400 adult Ethiopian wolves.

→ **IUCN Status:** Endangered

Claudio Sillero

→ **Education:** PhD from the University of Oxford, United Kingdom

→ **Nationality:** Argentine and British

→ **Organizational Affiliation:** Ethiopian Wolf Conservation Programme

→ **Years Working with Ethiopian Wolves:** 25

→ **Honors:** The Whitley Award for Animal Conservation from the Royal Geographical Society (1998)

→ **Books Published:** Coedited *The Biology and Conservation of Wild Canids* and *The Ethiopian Wolf: Status Survey and Conservation Action Plan*; coauthored the children's book *The Wolf Watchers*

→ **Notable Accomplishments:** Founded the Ethiopian Wolf Conservation Programme; senior research fellow at Oxford's Wildlife Conservation Research Unit; professor-at-large at the University of Vermont; chair of the IUCN Canid Specialist Group; head of conservation for the Born Free Foundation; Wildlife Conservation Network partner

WHO would think that the biggest threat to the most endangered wild canid in the world would be its own relative, the domestic dog? It is, however, true. "Dogs are closely related to Ethiopian wolves, but they are also a huge threat," says Dr. Claudio Sillero, the world's foremost authority on the Ethiopian wolf. "First they compete with them for their favorite prey: rodents. Second, male dogs will sometimes mate with female wolves and produce hybrid offspring, which dilute the wolves' already compromised gene pool. Third, and most worrisome, domestic dogs carry diseases such as rabies and canine distemper, which can infect a wolf population and cause catastrophic declines. Until we control the risks domestic dogs pose," he mourns, "these beautiful wolves I love will be in danger of extinction."

Sillero has been studying Ethiopian wolves for more than twenty-five years, and came to work with these animals through a mix of determination, fate, and luck. While growing up in Argentina, he

seriously considered a career in marine biology; however, after taking a trip to the Argentine cloud forest and having an up-close encounter with a mother jaguar and cubs, he set his mind on becoming a carnivore biologist. "I had always loved carnivores, but seeing those jaguars sealed it," he reflects. "I was going to focus my career on carnivores. In order to convince my family— and myself—that I was serious, I enrolled at the University of Nairobi in Kenya and studied spotted hyenas in the Aberdare Mountains. Then I had a fortuitous conversation over dinner with a New York Zoological Society biologist who was looking for someone to launch a study on what were at the time known as Simien foxes. That conversation changed my life forever. Ten days later I was in the Bale Mountains of Ethiopia, planning a study that would be the foundation of my career as an Ethiopian wolf specialist."

Of all the canid species, Ethiopian wolves are considered the rarest and most imperiled. There are about four hundred adults split into seven isolated populations—more than half of which are in the Bale Mountains, where Sillero started his work. But all the populations share the same Afroalpine habitat found above three thousand meters (nearly two miles) up in the Ethiopian highlands. "When I pictured myself doing carnivore research in Africa, I assumed I would be in a dry, hot savannah, following huge migrations of wildebeests and zebra, being stalked by lions and leopards. What I ended up doing was something entirely different," he said. "Instead I was riding horseback, bundled up in sweaters and down jackets, watching wolves ferret out giant mole rats for dinner."

The landscape where the Ethiopian wolves live is dominated by alpine meadows, green hills, and rocky terrain. These highlands experience dramatic temperature changes, easily swinging from hot afternoon temperatures with harsh sunlight, to zero degrees at night and frosty mornings coated with a thin

What You Should Know about Ethiopian Wolves

→ Sometimes misnomered Simien foxes or jackals, the species is more closely related to wolves and coyotes than to foxes or jackals.

→ Ethiopian wolves live in social packs with strict hierarchies, communal pup rearing, and territorial defense.

→ Despite living in highly socialized packs, they forage and feed individually on small prey.

→ Giant mole rats, grass rats, and Starck's hares make up the majority of the wolves' diet.

→ Ethiopian wolves sleep in the open, curled up into a ball, with their tails wrapped around their bodies.

Why It Is Important to Save the Ethiopian Wolf

Ethiopian wolves are a flagship species for the Afroalpine highlands of Ethiopia, which is a vital water source for the region and the lands below, including the world's longest river, the Nile.

The Ethiopian highlands are home to a vast abundance of small mammals living just below the surface. Grass rats, root rats, giant mole rats, and Starck's hares make up 96 percent of the diet of the Bale population of Ethiopian wolves studied by Sillero and his colleagues. "The highlands are a fantastic place to study predator/prey relationships," states Sillero. "The wolves are relatively tame, diurnal, and very visible. Some of my colleagues have spent years tracking and studying large carnivores without ever even seeing their subject. I was able to closely observe my wolves for over four thousand hours working on my PhD alone!"

Part of the reasons the wolves are so easy to study in the Bale Mountains is that wolves and local pastoralists are very tolerant of each other's presence, sharing the same meadows where the livestock graze and the wolves hunt rodents. And while overgrazing and conversion of land for crops is a threat to wolf populations in north Ethiopia, wolves in the Bale Mountain region have a relatively harmonious coexistence with the local people. Unfortunately, wherever there are shepherds, there are dogs, opening the door to interactions with the wolves, and disease transmission that has caused calamitous losses to past wolf populations.

"Whenever domestic dogs have brought outbreaks of rabies or canine distemper to an area, as many as three out of every four wolves have perished," Sillero reports. "With so few wolves in these mountains, one outbreak could wipe out an entire population. So we are trying to do something about it."

layer of snow. "These remarkable variations of temperature and weather are highly characteristic of Afroalpine habitat. We call it "the roof of Africa," says Sillero. "And while a cursory look may make a visitor think it has little life to offer, it in fact has a very high biomass and complex food chains." Species endemic to Ethiopia and found only in the Afroalpine highlands include the walia ibex, the mountain nyala, the gelada baboon, and fifteen species of birds, including the blue goose and the Northern wattled crane. Predators are numerous and varied in the highlands; in addition to the Ethiopian wolves—the only wolves found in all of Africa—there are honey badgers, golden jackals, leopards, spotted hyenas, servals, mongooses, and many raptors. These predator populations are well fed by the highland's most prolific and varied class of residents: rodents.

To address the threat, in 1995 Sillero started the Ethiopian Wolf Conservation Programme, and their vaccination campaign has inoculated more than sixty thousand dogs in the Ethiopian highlands to date. On two occasions he obtained special permission from the national government to intervene and vaccinate the wolves themselves. "We are currently testing an oral vaccine that would allow us to protect the whole Ethiopian wolf population before an outbreak. This is what we need to be doing. Once the outbreak hits, it is too late to save all the wolves." The shepherds, which also suffer livestock and human losses during rabies outbreaks, benefit from the proactive dog vaccinations as well. "The vaccination campaign helps the people and the wolves. It is a solution that everyone can be happy about."

In addition to spending decades devoted to the Ethiopian wolves, Sillero has expanded his expertise and credentials in broader carnivore conservation issues. For example, he is a senior research fellow at the University of Oxford's Wild-CRU (Wildlife Conservation Research Unit)—a collection of the world's top conservation biologists, working together to find solutions to conservation problems through scientific research. Sillero is also the chair of the IUCN's Canid Specialist Group, which is made up of leading canid specialists working jointly to address shared threats to wild dog, wolf, fox, and jackal species. Sillero and his wife, Dr. Jorgelina Marino, have also developed an online resource tool for carnivore practitioners, called the People and Wildlife Initiative. With a following of more than 650 wildlife

specialists, it provides a reservoir of reports and tool kits developed for conflict resolution.

But Ethiopian wolves remain Sillero's true focus, and he is optimistic about the future of the species, despite their scarcity and endangered status. "Although some of the populations are as small as ten or fifteen animals, the fact that Ethiopian wolf populations are spread out is good. The likelihood of them all being wiped out from a single ruinous event like a disease or a natural disaster is much less likely," says Sillero. "But such small populations require active management to ensure survival, and that is the stage we are currently at. If we can shift our efforts from reacting to threats, to instead proactively managing them—like providing vaccinations before a disease outbreak—Ethiopian wolves will be able to survive into the future."

NGUYEN VAN THAI
ASIAN PANGOLINS

"Pangolins comprise a large part of the illegal trade in Vietnam . . . An unbelievable 47.5 tons of pangolins were confiscated in Vietnam between 2005 and 2009."

Pangolins

→ **Species:** There are eight species of pangolins worldwide.

→ **Range:** Found in Southeast Asia—including both the mainland and adjacent islands—and Africa

→ **Population Trend:** Although there are no reliable population estimates for pangolins, there are reports of sharply declining numbers in many parts of their range, and all eight pangolin species are decreasing.

→ **IUCN Status:** The two species found in Vietnam, *Manis pentadactyla* and *Manis javanica* are Endangered. The other two Asian species and two of the African species are classified as Near Threatened.

Nguyen Van Thai

→ **Education:** Graduate certificate from the University of Kent, United Kingdom

→ **Nationality:** Vietnamese

→ **Organizational Affiliation:** Carnivore and Pangolin Conservation Program

→ **Years Working with Pangolins:** 7

→ **Notable Accomplishments:** Started Vietnam's first pangolin rescue and rehabilitation program; pioneered research on pangolin biology, health and behavior; selected for the Australian Development Scholarship program

NGUYEN Van Thai was just a young boy growing up in the primary forest areas of Northern Vietnam when he first became aware of his passion for wildlife and wild places. As most families in his village didn't have much, his neighbors often hunted for wild meat in the forests surrounding Cuc Phuong National Park. Thai recalls a scene from his childhood when he experienced firsthand the search and capture of the creatures with which he shared the forest. "I remember the first time I saw two people from my village digging out a pangolin burrow to catch the animals within. As I watched the juvenile climb onto the back of its mother, I was very sad knowing they were headed for the cooking pot." At that moment Thai knew what his future must be. He felt the need to protect the native wildlife he saw hunted and the forest he witnessed being degraded and destroyed. He hoped he could change the views and actions of his own people.

Asian pangolins—the small animals that inspired Thai to pursue a career very different from most Vietnamese—are sometimes called "scaly anteaters." They are highly desired across many parts of Asia for their meat and scales, and demand has only increased with the growing sector of Asian

threatened, they typically roll into a ball, which may protect them from some predators, but not from humans. Pangolin and other illegal wildlife shipments are often comprised of some combination of frozen meat, live animals, and scales or other parts. When they are discovered alive, they are found stuffed into mesh bags tied at the top and thrown into boxes. There may be dozens, or hundreds, of animals that need care—and very few facilities equipped to handle them. Even after being confiscated by authorities, most pangolins are sold right back into the black market due to lack of options and places to care for them, which only reinforces the participants' engagement in this criminal business. "We've got to stop all this from continuing," implores Thai.

After attending forestry school, one of the only avenues to an environmental career in Vietnam, Thai applied at a newly opened rescue center for small carnivores near his home outside Cuc Phuong National Park. Just a few years after his first experience with the mom and baby pangolin, these small, defenseless animals could no longer be found in the nearby forests. They had been hunted out. His first order of business: start a program to help pangolins survive. Thai set up the country's first pangolin research and rescue center with little money and support. But it was enough. A veterinarian from Australia came to help, and donors, mostly from zoos around the world, pitched in. The Carnivore and Pangolin Conservation Program (CPCP) was born. Now when authorities caught a person smuggling live pangolins, they had a place to bring survivors.

middle class who can now afford to buy food and medicines made from exotic animals. As a result, pangolin populations have declined drastically across their range in Southeast Asia.

Though pangolins today are protected by law, these vulnerable animals are commercially hunted in huge numbers wherever they can still be found. Not only do they appear on some restaurant menus, but their scales are used in traditional Asian medicines. "Pangolins comprise a large part of the illegal trade in Vietnam," says Thai, "mostly smuggled across the border from Cambodia or Laos, or coming by boat from farther away, and often on their way to China, where the demand is greatest." Of the eight pangolin species, two are found in Vietnam—and both are endangered.

Pangolins are nocturnal, tree-climbing, toothless mammals found in both Asia and Africa. When

When Thai started the pangolin rescue center, not much was known about how to care for healthy pangolins, much less treat traumatized ones. But Thai learned as he went: "It was a big challenge for me because there is so little information about pangolins," he says. "When the first three animals arrived from the authorities, I spent a lot of time just figuring out how to keep them alive." Ants were the logical diet, but what kind—and did they need anything else? The wild pangolin diet is still being studied, but it appears that weaver ants are one of the pangolin's favorite foods. Its long, thin tongue laps in and out dozens of times per minute, its sticky saliva trapping the ants and pulling them into the small toothless mouth. Pangolins have been estimated to eat up to five thousand ants per feeding. This number of ants per night can become a problem for a rescue center unless there happens to be an unlimited quantity nearby, which even in a forest area is unlikely. To create a sustainable supply, Thai attended a course in ant farming and has since set up about forty colonies in nearby fruit farms and inside the national park. "We hope the farms will become the main source of natural food for our pangolins. But part of our aim is to also develop a nutritious artificial diet as well, to help reduce the demand for a constant supply of live ants."

One of the CPCP's objectives is to get more of the pangolins to rescue centers without resale back to the trade, so Thai and his team have taught rangers to distinguish between the two Vietnamese species, instructed them on their endangered status, and provided information about placement of confiscated animals. Rangers also learn how to handle and care for the animals they obtain until they can be placed or released. Following the CPCP's lead, there are now two other pangolin rescue sites in Vietnam, and Thai shares expertise and information with them regularly.

He is also figuring out ways to improve the general management and care of pangolins after confiscation. In order to get a

What You Should Know about Pangolins

→ Pangolin scales are made of keratin, just like human fingernails.

→ Baby pangolins ride at the base of the broad, long tail of their mother.

→ Pangolins are sometimes called "scaly anteaters"; however, they are not true anteaters, but a taxonomically distinct species.

→ As the number of pangolins declines while demand stays high, the price paid to poachers increases, which leads to even higher rates of illegal trade, the largest threat to pangolins in the wild.

complete picture, he and a student "went nocturnal" for two months. After much recording of data, behavior, lunar cycles, temperature, and humidity, Thai now has a better idea of the pangolin's needs. Many, especially Thai's boyhood neighbors, may find it surprising that rescued pangolins benefit from environmental enrichment—things to keep them stimulated, active, and challenged while they recuperate. Thai's study also suggested improvements for enclosure design and husbandry, which Thai plans to implement, as well as doing more research in this area.

The overall goal, however, of Thai's work is to prevent pangolins from being poached in the first place. When contemplating this problem, the question he had was, "How can pangolins be so common in the illegal trade when they are so rarely seen by researchers and biologists trying to study the animals?" To find out the answer, Thai interviewed hunters to learn more about pangolins, their habits, and how to catch the animals. The study showed Thai that in order to conserve Vietnamese pangolins, hunting dogs need to be banned and wire snare traps removed from the forests. Researchers must continue to learn more about where pangolins live and what their needs are in the wild, and, perhaps most important, he needed to raise awareness about the pangolins' plight, to reduce market demand among native Vietnamese.

One of Thai's most rewarding moments was when one of his original rescued pangolins gave birth to a member of the next generation of scaly anteaters. "Many people in Vietnam see the value of wildlife only in terms of consumption. I always show how much I care for and love the animals we work to save. Some people say that I am crazy, but many people start to think about wildlife in different ways—that maybe there is a value to conservation. I think that, perhaps, we are making progress."

Why It Is Important to Save Pangolins

Pangolins play a critical role in natural insect control, especially ants and termites, saving humans millions of dollars to pest damage and reducing the need for harmful chemical pesticides. Additionally, pangolin burrows provide shelter for many species, such as rodents and reptiles.

LAURIE MARKER
CHEETAH

"We're showing that good livestock management means that farmers and predators can live together . . . Cheetahs and farmers can coexist."

WHEN Laurie Marker gave up her life in the United States twenty years ago to save cheetahs in Africa, she had no idea she would eventually be selling firewood, certifying beef, and breeding dogs—all in the name of cheetah conservation. But this wide range of innovative conservation schemes is a testament to her adaptive and highly successful approach to conservation. "It's all about being there on the ground and identifying what the real problems are," says Marker. "That's where you find the many different solutions that can work. Not only for the cheetahs but also for the people who live beside them."

Marker's life with cheetahs began in 1974 when she took a job at a wildlife park in Oregon, running the veterinary clinic. Almost immediately she took over the care of the ten cheetahs at the park, but realized that very little was known about the animals' biology, ecology, and status in the wild. "I began writing scientists around the world, asking for even basic information about cheetahs. What I found was a large community also looking for answers to the same questions. How could so little be known about this animal that people had revered and worked with for over five thousand years?" asked Marker. "I was fascinated."

So Marker decided to go to Africa and look for answers to her questions head-on. At the end of the nineteenth century, cheetahs numbered near one hundred thousand. Retaliatory killing from human-cheetah conflict, loss of habitat and prey base, competition with larger predators, and inbreeding caused the global population of cheetahs to drop as low as ten thousand animals. What Marker found was that the world's fastest land mammal was clearly in crisis.

In 1991, knowing more now about the situation, Marker decided to settle in Namibia, the country with the largest population of wild cheetahs, and cofounded the Cheetah Conservation Fund (CCF). She developed a three-pronged strategy for CCF, employing research, conservation, and education in order to turn around the cheetah's decline.

Seeing firsthand that retaliatory killings of cheetahs by farmers was a significant problem in Namibia, Marker began breeding and donating Anatolian Shepherd dogs in 1994, and then later Kangal dogs, to guard livestock from cheetahs. The program began modestly, with one litter a year being placed on local farms. Since then the initiative has skyrocketed, with more than 370 dogs born and placed, and a long waiting list of farmers hoping to receive one of Marker's dogs. "It really works," she says. "After the dogs have been placed, farmers are seeing their losses from all predators—cheetahs, caracals, jackals, even leopards—reduced to almost zero." Guard dogs—and guard donkeys, for that matter—

are an active deterrent to predators. Cheetahs and other carnivores look for the easiest meal possible, so a potential injury from a fight with a guard animal is typically enough of a disincentive for a predator to move on to another meal instead.

The livestock guard dog program evolved into training local farmers and ranchers in a wide variety of best practices that allow for a shared environment with native wildlife. Says Marker, "We're showing that good livestock management means farmers and predators can live together. I grew up on a farm and understand farmers' struggles, but cheetahs and farmers can coexist." CCF has now trained thousands of African farmers in wildlife management and husbandry practices that make the most sense for successful livestock and still maintain a diverse ecosystem.

In 2000, Marker and her team of local workers and international volunteers built the Cheetah Research and Education Center, which includes a state-of-the-art veterinary and genetic laboratory and the world's only cheetah history museum. Since opening, the Center has received more than fifty thousand visitors, including local citizens, schoolchildren, and travelers. The Center also demonstrates model livestock and agricultural farming operations, and a cheetah rescue center that serves as a holding facility for cheetahs needing relocation due to conflict with humans, or a long-term home for orphaned cheetahs that cannot be reintroduced into the wild.

Marker has also developed a number of innovative microenterprises that not only help cheetahs

prosper, but also bring income to local residents. She created a business that selectively harvests thickened thornbushes responsible for bush encroachment, a form of desertification that is crowding out important cheetah grassland habitat. CCF works with locals to harvest these pest bushes and convert them into fuel logs known as "Bushbloks." The process reclaims cheetah habitat and employs local people in a sustainable industry, while supplying a Forest Stewardship Council–certified product that takes pressure off of Africa's disappearing native forests and is an alternative to charcoal. And more recently, Marker and her team have been working toward a cheetah-friendly certified beef initiative, called Cheetah Country Beef. The certified program will provide financial

Why It Is Important to Save Cheetahs

As the fastest apex land predator, the cheetah helps control prey levels of those species that can outrun other predators. They also keep the prey populations healthy by weeding out the sick, weak, and slow. Finally, cheetah kills provide for scavengers, such as vultures, hyenas, and jackals.

incentives and an eco-friendly label for farmers who practice predator-friendly livestock management techniques.

With these numerous successful conservation programs, CCF has continued to grow and now provides guidance and assistance to Botswana, Kenya, South Africa, Iran, Algeria, Zimbabwe, and Angola. "Every time I go into a new place where cheetahs live," says Marker, "I find out what the problems are for cheetahs by conducting a needs assessment. Then I find the right on-the-ground partners. Lastly I look for solutions—evaluating earlier models and efforts, and adapting them for this new spot."

Marker is part of a team investigating the feasibility of reestablishing a population of cheetahs to India, where they have been extinct for sixty years. "We've identified suitable habitat, and we're working with the government of India to make it happen." Today there are only cheetahs in Africa and a small pocket of about a hundred cheetahs in Iran, where CCF is also working. "Wouldn't it be amazing to bring cheetahs back to another part of Asia in our lifetime?"

Marker has real hope for the cheetah, as despite their many threats, they have shown a resilience and ability to survive throughout history. Cheetahs are the oldest of the big cats and can readily adapt to their environment. For example the long-legged, short-haired cheetahs of the Sahara desert are genetically very similar but very different looking from the longer-haired cheetahs found in the milder climate of Namibia.

Marker observes, "The desert cheetahs make the cheetahs in my part of the world look more like snow leopards."

Although she has now been immersed in the world of cheetah conservation for more than thirty-five years, Marker still encounters surprises. In 2010 she received a call from a landowner in Angola, claiming to have seen cheetahs near his property. After a three-decade war, the scientific community had generally given up on the possibility of healthy wildlife populations—much less apex predators—surviving in the country. But Marker decided to go anyway and look for the unlikely signs of cheetahs. To her amazement she actually saw two cheetahs on her first survey out into Angola wilderness. "I don't know if the animals had emigrated from northern Namibia, or if they had held on during the long conflict, but they were there. So were oryx and springbok, and other cheetah prey that had made a comeback in the past few years. It was thrilling!"

"The cheetah is the most amazing animal. It equals anything as exciting as dinosaurs." Says Marker, "Nothing in the world can equal its speed, build, or adaptations. But right now it's running its most important race—for survival. The challenges are huge: rising populations, high levels of poverty, few wildlife protected areas where cheetahs survive, and shrinking wilderness. But with commitment, bigger partners, and bigger plans that pull together the best conservation and economic models, I think we can still win."

IAIN DOUGLAS-HAMILTON
AFRICAN ELEPHANTS

"The threat of poaching for ivory has again reached alarming proportions for most elephants in Africa. It is spelling disaster for elephant way of life, if not their very existence. I fear we need another wake-up call."

African Elephants

→ **Scientific Name:** Savannah, *Loxodonta africana*; Forest, *Loxodonta cyclotis*

→ **Range:** Found across sub-Saharan Africa, in diverse environments from savannah to forest to desert

→ **Population Trend:** It is estimated that between 1980 and 1990 the population of African elephants was more than halved, from 1.3 million to approximately 600,000. The number of elephants is increasing in protected areas of East and South Africa but declining in Central and West Africa.

→ **IUCN Status:** Vulnerable

Iain Douglas-Hamilton

→ **Education:** DPhil from Oxford University, United Kingdom

→ **Nationality:** British

→ **Organizational Affiliation:** Save the Elephants

→ **Years Working with African Elephants:** Nearly 50

→ **Honors:** Recipient of the Indianapolis Prize (2010); received the Disney Conservation Legacy Award (2006); made an officer of the Order of the British Empire (1993); received the Order of the Golden Ark (1988)

→ **Books Published:** *Among the Elephants* and *Battle for the Elephants* (coauthored with his wife, Oria)

→ **Notable Accomplishments:** First to alert the world to the elephant poaching holocaust; instrumental in bringing about the global ivory trade ban; founded Save the Elephants, Wildlife Conservation Network partner

IAIN Douglas-Hamilton sees the world through the eyes of the elephant—he feels he must if he's to help them survive. Douglas-Hamilton has studied, protected, and taught about elephants for most of his life. He was the first to gain attention for the massive slaughter of elephants supplying the 1970s ivory trade. After all the years he has worked to learn about the incredible social behavior, movements, and threats to this intelligent herbivore, his biggest challenge is still securing their future.

"The survival of elephants depends upon the behavior of humans," he says, "both those who live with them and those who don't. We all play a part in the solutions." Douglas-Hamilton has spent his life showing the way—he has not just been committed to an unrelenting war against poaching; he has also engaged in human-elephant conflict resolutions. The elephant is the largest land mammal on Earth, but this has only made its situation more precarious. Elephants need vast amounts of food, water, minerals, and space in order to sustain themselves. With human population growing and resources becoming scarcer, conflict between elephants and people—the two dominant forces in the African landscape—is

escalating. In 1993, Douglas-Hamilton founded an organization called Save the Elephants, dedicated to securing a future for elephants and their habitats and to encouraging a peaceful coexistence between humans and elephants. The solutions range from high-tech to amazingly "natural." Douglas-Hamilton feels he must investigate them all to find the right fix for each situation.

One of the more recent projects that Save the Elephants is testing is the placing of collars on "problem" elephants. These collars will text messages about the animals' location. Obtaining this information well ahead of the animals entering areas where humans live and grow their crops will provide a greater understanding of how to head off the elephants before damage—and conflict—arises. On the opposite end of the technology spectrum is an idea being studied utilizing a natural antagonist of the elephant—honey bees. Lucy King, who works as a head scientist for Douglas-Hamilton and Save the Elephants, heads up this project. She goes out and places beehives at regular intervals around a garden plot or village boundry, then monitors the local elephants' behaviors. The hives are attached to each other by wire. If elephants try to break through the wire, the disturbed bees become angry and swarm the elephants, which then flee. "Interestingly, what we've found out is that often just the presence of the hives is enough to make the elephants steer clear—it's been a great success in smaller areas needing protection," says Douglas-Hamilton.

African elephants are found in thirty-seven countries and an amazing variety of habitat types, from desert to mountains and forest to savannas. Because African elephants range so far and wide over such a vast continent, it has been virtually impossible to determine their exact density. Douglas-Hamilton originated the African Elephant Specialist Group in the mid-1970s that all across Africa monitors elephant populations and death—both natural and otherwise. During the '70s and '80s elephants were facing massive poaching, as well as habitat loss and fragmentation.

What You Should Know about African Elephants

→ African elephants are the largest terrestrial animal on Earth.

→ Forest elephants of Central Africa are now being scientifically considered a separate species.

→ Elephant herds are led by the dominant female, who takes responsibility for the safety and survival of the entire group.

→ When the dominant female dies or is killed, her eldest daughter is most likely to take over leadership.

Why It Is Important to Save Elephants

Elephants shape the environments in which they live by opening up forests, controlling brush and tree growth, and digging for water and minerals, which benefits other animals. Their copious amounts of dung also help fertilize the landscape and disperse seeds.

Douglas-Hamilton estimated that the number of elephants on the African continent was halved between 1979 and 1989. Kenya lost as much as 85 percent of their elephant population during this time when poaching was at its worst. "Unfortunately the threat of poaching for ivory in 2011 has again reached alarming proportions for most elephants in Africa. Growing prosperity in certain regions of the world, especially Asia, and increased demand in the U.S. as well, has pushed up prices, making the illegal market even more profitable. Add to that conflict-related deaths, animals killed for meat, and continuing habitat and resource loss, and it is spelling disaster for elephant way of life, if not their very existence, in many areas of Africa," points out Douglas-Hamilton. "I fear we need another wake-up call."

In order to make available as much accurate, timely information as possible about what's happening day to day concerning elephants in range countries, Save the Elephants sponsors an online news service to provide access to research papers, news articles, and other reports to anyone interested. Douglas-Hamilton believes this link is fundamental. "Connecting people who want to help make a difference for elephants is imperative. No one can solve this alone."

In fact, the Douglas-Hamiltons have made wildlife and conservation a family affair. Oria, Iain's wife, owns and runs an ecologically minded safari lodge in Samburu, Elephant Watch Safari, where Save the Elephants is based. Their children, Saba and Mara Moon, nicknamed Dudu (or "insect" in Kiswahili), because she was always buzzing around, are both deeply involved in outreach efforts educating the world about African wildlife and people. Douglas-Hamilton and his wife have also authored two authoritative books on elephants: *Among the Elephants* and *Battle for the Elephants*. In recognition of his years of study and work on behalf of elephants, Douglas-Hamilton was awarded one of conservation's highest honors, Order of the Golden Ark, and one of the largest conservation awards, the Indianapolis Prize, in 2010.

"My life and my family are all intertwined with elephants and Africa," states Douglas-Hamilton. "I can't imagine a world without vast herds of elephants shaping the landscape as they have for centuries. We all need to do everything we can to make sure that continues. Africa would be such a different and less spectacular continent without them."

WATER

WORKING IN THE OCEANS AND RIVERS

CHAPTER INTRODUCTION

BY TED DANSON, AWARD-WINNING ACTOR, OCEAN
ADVOCATE, AND OCEANA BOARD MEMBER

Every Piece Matters

I have great respect for wildlife conservationists.
Most of my efforts personally have been to protect
the habitat, which hopefully then saves the critters,
like penguins, octopuses, dolphins, corals, and everything else in the ocean that I also care about. By
keeping the water and the fish stocks healthy—keeping the oceans vital—the entire ecosystem keeps
working as it is meant to.

I grew up in Arizona, about as far from oceans
as you can get. My favorite times as a child were
when my family would visit relatives in Southern
California. We would rent a cottage, and all the
cousins would hang out at the beach all day long.
Because I came from the desert, it was like a pil-
grimage—I loved experiencing the ocean. Everyone
in my family, no matter what age, found something
to do that gave them joy at the ocean.

One day much later, in my early thirties, I was
walking with daughters Kate and Alexis on a beach in
Santa Monica. We came across a sign saying, "Water Is
Polluted, No Swimming." Try as I might, I could not
explain to them why something so beautiful and vast
as the ocean could be polluted enough for them to be
kept from enjoying it. Around that same time, I was
involved with a neighborhood group trying to prevent
an oil company from digging oil wells on a local beach.
These experiences made me want to do more to protect the ocean that I cared about so deeply, so I joined
with an environmental lawyer, and we formed an
organization called the American Oceans Campaign.
We worked out of a garage, and slowly grew. In 2002
we merged with the group Oceana, and we are now
the largest ocean conservation group focused exclusively on the oceans of the world. And what makes the
work of Oceana so exciting is that what is happening

107

to our oceans right now is an environmental disaster that can be averted. Things are bad right now, but this is something that can be turned around.

So just how bad are things? In 2000 a study discovered that since 1988, more and more boats going out are bringing back fewer and fewer fish. For the first time in human history, worldwide fish catch has gone down. I grew up in the '50s, and since then, 90 percent of the tuna around back then are gone—fished out. Ninety percent of the sharks, swordfish, marlin, and king mackerel are all gone. The top predators—the lions and tigers of the ocean—are gone since the days when I was a kid visiting the beach with my family. The Food and Agriculture Organization of the United Nations says that 85 percent of the world's fisheries are fully or overfished. You can see that we are heading toward collapsing the vitality of our oceans unless we change our ways. It is not hyperbole to say we are overstressing our oceans to the point that they could conceivably collapse.

Most people think, *There are so many species in the ocean, what would it matter if we lose a few here and there? Why care about sharks, for example?* Humans kill more than 100 million sharks a year—mostly for shark fin soup, considered a sign of prosperity in some places of the world. The practice is not only unsustainable, but barbaric and wasteful—finning sharks and sinking them alive, not even using their meat as food. But who cares?

We should. Off the East Coast, fishers wiped out local shark populations because of unsustainable fishing and finning. Soon after, the North Carolina scallop industry collapsed. Turns out that the sharks had kept the ray population down naturally. Without sharks, the rays ate way too many scallops. Messing around with the food chain has consequences that can't be foreseen. We can collapse the entire system by throwing it out of whack. Ocean biodiversity is just like the rainforest: it is so complicated and interwoven that if you wipe out a piece, you have an impact. That's what happens.

So it's not only about the amazement of being able to see a breaching orca, or a great white shark fin piercing the surface—which is good for our souls—but it's about keeping the ecological balance, and the importance of sustainably maintaining the economic benefits, and also our moral obligation to other life on the planet. There are so many reasons to take care of the oceans and the critters in them.

What the marine scientists, and the wildlife conservationists and ocean advocates, tell us is that this is fixable. This is doable. Fish populations are incredibly resilient. The ocean can rebound. Positive things can happen and are happening in some places. We can solve this if we choose to. The political will is beginning to be there. So if you want to do something about this, do it with a light heart. If you are overwhelmed and are overly sad or frustrated, you won't succeed. Try to stay lighthearted. Saving species is fun. How exciting that you have the ability to save something in this lifetime.

So go to the coastline, the beach, or even just watch a beach movie. Find the joy in the ocean. Then go have a delicious piece of wild, sustainably caught fish. And enjoy the hell out it. Then get in touch with how much you enjoy the ocean. Commit to conserving the ocean. And do it from a place of lightheartedness. That is the real way to make a difference.

BRENT STEWART
WHALE SHARK

"Virtually everything that might be learned about whale sharks could be key to the eventual conservation of them and their ocean habitats."

Whale Shark

→ **Scientific Name:** *Rhincodon typus*

→ **Range:** All tropical and warm temperate oceans and coastal areas around the globe, except for the Mediterranean

→ **Population Trend:** Relatively unknown abundance and uncertain trends

→ **IUCN Status:** Vulnerable

Brent Stewart

→ **Education:** JD from Boalt Hall School of Law at the University of California, Berkeley, and PhD from the University of California, Los Angeles

→ **Nationality:** American

→ **Organizational Affiliation:** Hubbs-SeaWorld Research Institute

→ **Years Working with Whale Sharks:** 30

→ **Honors:** Explorer's Club Lowell Thomas Award (2011); Fellow of the Royal Geographical Society (2000); national fellow of the Explorers Club (1991)

→ **Books Published:** Coauthored *National Audubon Society Guide to Marine Mammals of the World* and *Walker's Marine Mammals of the World.*

→ **Notable Accomplishments:** Served at the U.S. Department of State as a science fellow and as diplomacy fellow of the American Association for the Advancement of Science.

AS a grad student, Brent Stewart had the chance to work on a variety of projects that would make just about any marine biologist jealous. They ranged from dolphin detection and avoidance of fishing nets to surveying bowhead whale populations in the Beaufort Sea and studies of beluga whales in Bristol Bay. His thesis was on seal ecology and population demographics in the Channel Islands, which he still keeps up with today. And it was in the late 1970s that Stewart first developed his great lifelong interest in whale sharks. His fascination was piqued when he realized that surprisingly little was known about such large creatures. "The intrigue for me was that they were not easily found and not often observable," he said. "That provoked even more curiosity, as whale sharks are filter feeders, on small phytoplankton and zooplankton, so they might be expected to spend most of their time relatively near the ocean surface—where they should presumably be more often seen."

In the early '80s, Stewart helped two other researchers working at the Hubbs-SeaWorld Research Institute compile what little information

What You Should Know about Whale Sharks

→ Whale sharks are the world's largest fish, capable of reaching over 45 feet in length.

→ Despite being the largest fish, they consume the smallest prey—phyotoplankton, fish eggs and larvae, krill, and sometimes small schooling fishes—by gulping large amounts of water and then filtering it through their gill rakers.

→ Few adult females have been seen. Only one pregnant whale shark has ever been caught, with 300 pups ready to be born.

→ It may take 30 years for whale shark offspring to mature.

→ Hunting of whale sharks has been banned in many countries, though enforcement of those bans is difficult, if possible at all.

→ Poaching and "finning"—removal of fins from free-ranging sharks—continue in some areas.

there was about the species. That effort solidified his commitment to finding out more. "The sense of discovery is one of the most exciting things and among the greatest rewards in science. It was probably the most compelling aspect about trying to study whale sharks . . . that virtually everything that might be learned about them would be grand discovery, and any new information could be key to the eventual conservation of them and their ocean habitats."

The situation is a bit paradoxical, according to Stewart. "The double-edged sword in studying a species like the whale shark is that one of the key motivations for studying them—that there is so little known about the species—is also a major drawback when it comes to convincing potential supporters and other scientists that you can actually find the sharks and work with them." But that's what Stewart has done—on all counts and for more than three decades—which has added important information to our knowledge of the species. Stewart is known around the globe as "the go-to guy" if you want to know more about sea life—where it goes, how deep it dives, how long it spends below the surface, and even who is related to whom. But it is whale sharks on which Stewart has zeroed in his attention and his dart gun, with which he attaches specially designed data-gathering tags. These tags transmit information regarding how long the animals spend at the surface, how deep they dive, how far they travel, and where they go—the most basic biology and life history of the largest fish on Earth. Stewart travels regularly to the farthest corners of the planet—the Maldives, off the coast of Africa, to the Philippines and Western Australia—to tag his subjects and gather his data. "Since starting work at Hubbs-SeaWorld Research Institute," he says, "I've spent at least seven to eight months a year away from the office and my home, at various field sites around the world." The information Stewart obtains is vital to protecting the future of this giant fish.

Thanks in part to Stewart's satellite tags and subsequent data analysis, what has now been discovered about whale sharks only

adds to the intrigue of the species. These sharks are thought to be able to reach over forty-five feet long, although average length appears to be between twenty and thirty-three feet. They have huge, gaping mouths filled with approximately three thousand tiny teeth, not even used for feeding. Whale sharks are filter feeders, meaning they literally suck in tons of salt water along with *plankton*, small drifting plants and animals in the seas, then strain out the water and swallow the nutritious foodstuff. Stewart and colleagues have found whale sharks to be highly mobile, with one tagged animal having traveled more than eight thousand miles over the course of three years, though there is no solid evidence for true migrations.

Two of the main threats to sharks worldwide, shark fishing and *finning*—the removal of just the fins from live sharks to supply a growing demand for shark fin soup, mainly in Asia—have caused substantial declines of many shark species. One of the reasons sharks, including the whale shark, are so vulnerable to extinction, and why some shark populations have already declined by up to 90 percent, is that many sharks grow slowly, mature later

Why It Is Important to Save Whale Sharks

Whale sharks appear to be important animals in the ecology of coral reefs and also near surface and deepwater offshore habitats. Important and substantial ecotourism industries have developed in many areas of the Indian Ocean, Indonesia, and the Caribbean to allow tourists to approach and swim with whale sharks. These local communities now depend on the seasonal appearance of whale sharks in their waters for tourist income.

in life, have long gestation periods, and bear few young. In fact, it has been speculated that whale sharks do not become sexually mature until around thirty years old—very late in life for most animals. Losing mature animals to fishermen's nets, finning, or depleted food availability can easily erode reproductive success for such slow-reproducing species.

The fact that the whale shark was until recently listed on the World Conservation Union's Red List of Threatened Species as "Data Deficient" is the very reason Stewart's work is so critical. This category relates to species suspected to be endangered, vulnerable, or rare, but about which there is too little known to support a rational assessment of abundance and status. With additional information regarding populations, threats, and biology provided by Stewart and others who are studying the colossal shark, the Convention on International Trade in Endangered Species of Wild Fauna and Flora (or CITES) proposed new global protections for whale sharks in 2002 by making them the first shark species, along with the basking shark, to be protected by CITES' international trade controls. Even so, these large fish are still threatened with population declines, given their vulnerability.

In comparison with terrestrial vertebrates, whale sharks and other marine species are difficult subjects on which to collect quantitative population and life history data. Stewart states, "There are important concerns about what kinds of studies can be realistically done at sea and what kinds of equipment and technologies might be applied to produce substantive data about whale shark biology, ecology, biogeography, foraging ecology, and physiology. I am always looking to discover better ways to obtain this necessary information to help protect this species."

Stewart also knows he must understand the people and politics of the regions in which whale sharks are found if there is to be support for their conservation. Exposure to diverse cultures, points of view, environments, and international wildlife species has had important influences on his thinking about conservation issues and the complexities of human responses to differing needs. According to Stewart, "the truths are rarely pure and never simple."

Stewart has always striven to figure out ways to make wildlife conservation workable to society as a whole, with all its differing interests, rule making, and political priorities. Obtaining a law degree in addition to his science doctorate provided him with additional tools to address these complex issues. He was able to put his education and interest in biology, conservation, and the law to use when he was selected by the American Association for the Advancement of Science to serve as a science and diplomacy fellow at the U.S. Department of State. "During the period I spent in Washington, D.C., my work included coming full circle, back to the issues that had given me my first experience with marine animals many years ago, but this time in a national and international policy context. Now I want to use all my experiences, knowledge, and skills to help conserve and ensure the survival of the biggest fish on Earth."

GERALD KOOYMAN
EMPEROR PENGUIN

"Antarctica is the coldest, driest, windiest continent on Earth. Most people would have problems working there, but for me, the animals and my work are so stimulating that it is worth the discomforts."

Emperor Penguin

→ **Scientific Name:** *Aptenodytes forsteri*

→ **Range:** Circumpolar Antarctic

→ **Population Trend:** Appears stable at approximately 400,000 individuals; however, this species is being considered for inclusion on the U.S. Endangered Species List due to possible reduced food availability and climate change.

→ **IUCN Status:** Least Concern

Gerald Kooyman

→ **Education:** PhD from the University of Arizona

→ **Nationality:** American

→ **Organizational Affiliation:** Scripps Institution of Oceanography

→ **Years Working with Emperor Penguins:** Almost 45

→ **Honors:** The Quadrennial Finn Ronne Award, the Explorers Club, NYC (2007); the first Kenneth Norris Life Time Achievement Award of the Marine Mammal Society (2005); Special Creativity Award, National Science Foundation (1991); Kooyman Peak in Queen Elizabeth Range, Antarctica, named after Gerald Kooyman (1966); Antarctica Medal (1963)

→ **Books Published:** *Weddell Seal: Consummate Diver*; *Fur Seals: Maternal Strategies on Land and at Sea*; *Diverse Divers: Physiology and Behavior*

→ **Notable Accomplishments:** Designed and developed the first time/depth recorder; world authority on emperor penguins who has brought attention to the threat of climate change on penguin populations

GERALD Kooyman began a very "cool" career by studying the diving physiology of marine mammals such as the Weddell seal in the freezing waters of the Southern Hemisphere. He then became intrigued with arguably the greatest ambassador of the Antarctic—the emperor penguin. While it may seem strange to focus on two such distinct species, there are surprising similarities. Both animals are mid-level predators that prey on many of the same species, and both have incredible deep-dive capabilities. "The emperor penguin and the Weddell seal are the two warm-blooded animals best adapted to polar life, and they are the only ones who stay all year round. A more common survival strategy is to leave locations during the harshest times of the year, but not these two," states Kooyman.

Kooyman actually designed and developed the first time/depth recorder (TDR) to measure diving capabilities of animals such as seals and penguins.

Prior to this instrument, the only dive information available was from forced submersions of animals in water-filled tubs or pools, or from those caught in traps or on fishing lines. "My first incredible experience with the emperor penguin was in 1967, from a newly employed underwater observation chamber still in use today," says Kooyman. "I immediately suspected this largest of penguin species had some remarkable diving capabilities. I was right!" Kooyman felt a surge of excitement when he retrieved the first wild, free-diving penguin results and discovered that dive depths were often greater than 400 meters, and some dives exceeded eighteen minutes in length. Later records with a much larger sample size resulted in dives as deep as 550 meters (over 1,800 feet). Kooyman has been studying the emperor penguin ever since, and his research has provided a substantial share of the existing knowledge about emperors from the field. For example, when it was thought that the penguins stayed relatively close to their home colony sites, he showed for the first time that these flightless birds travel over large areas to find food.

One of Kooyman's most exhilarating research expeditions involved three days spent with three companions, snowmobiling over rough, glacial terrain to reach a remote colony of emperor penguins at Cape Washington. Sixteen thousand pairs of emperors thrived there at that time, and upon arrival several hundred of them came around to explore the men's camp. Kooyman recalls what happened when a team from *Good Morning America* flew in to do a story from their campsite. The birds, curious about these newcomers, lined up to "greet" the crew. Even as Kooyman prepared for and taped the interview, he was upstaged by the penguins, who ultimately received more airtime than the scientist did.

Emperor penguins are the largest of eighteen penguin species, which breed and live virtually year-round on sea ice.

What You Should Know about Penguins

→ There are 18 species of penguins, found primarily in Antarctica, Australia, New Zealand, South America, and South Africa.

→ The emperor penguin is the only penguin species that breeds during the Antarctic winter, the coldest time and place on Earth.

→ The emperor penguin is serially monogamous, staying faithful to its chosen mate during each breeding season but potentially choosing a new mate the following year. Studies show that about 15 percent keep the same mate the next year.

→ Since most emperor colonies breed on ice, not land, the chicks' fledging must correspond with the melting of the ice.

They stand approximately three feet tall and can eat as much as twelve pounds of food a day going into the breeding season. Males fast during the entire courtship, breeding, and incubation periods—an astounding total of between 90 and 120 days. Each female lays only one egg, so all the energy and parental effort are spent on that one offspring. The timing of hatching seems particularly harsh, as the chick emerges in the coldest part of the year, when temperatures can be as low as –50 degrees Fahrenheit. The chick is about five inches tall at hatching and fits into a warm envelope of skin and feathers on the adults' bellies. All this occurs so that the chick is ready to be on his own at the beginning of summer, a warmer, more plentiful season. Even so, the months between birth and maturity are filled with perils, and many hatchlings don't make it through the first year.

"Antarctica is the coldest, driest, windiest continent on Earth. Most people would have problems working there, but for me," says Kooyman, "the animals and my work are so stimulating that it is worth the discomforts. The excitement of exploration and discovery is thrilling and gratifying, but it only comes with lots of planning, effort, and teamwork." None of that happens by chance. In fact, Kooyman began preparing his sons at young ages for the rigors of field research in one of the most forbidding places on Earth. "My son Carsten became an important member of the research dive team, and my son Tory managed the camp, equipment, and vehicles. It's really a special feeling to rely on your family and colleagues in potentially hazardous situations." This is one of the things that draws Kooyman to work on this remote continent—the bonds and closeness formed when people share such extreme conditions and close quarters. Kooyman is munificent concerning the accomplishments of other professionals, which have all led to a greater understanding of a species threatened by climate change and shifting icebergs.

Kooyman's latest trips to Antarctica have documented climactic changes to the emperor penguins' habitat. In fact, in 2001 Kooyman and his colleagues witnessed the most destructive force he'd seen. That year, the largest iceberg ever recorded drifted, collided with, and eventually destroyed one of Kooyman's study sites—an emperor breeding colony. Five years later, chick production was still only a third of what it was the year before the collapse. "Penguin populations have historically risen and fallen depending on several factors, such as sea ice stability," says Kooyman. Emperor penguins are dependent on fast ice remaining thick and frozen. If the ice melts too fast and breaks up early, chicks won't survive.

"When I first began studying animals in such remote locations almost fifty years ago, I thought nothing would ever touch them. Now I know there is no place unaffected by humans—and we must be the ones to help preserve the penguins and other species—or my grandchildren may never be able to see the incredible sights and animals that I have been fortunate enough to see."

Why It Is Important to Save Emperor Penguins

Emperor penguins have adapted to exist year-round in one of the most inhospitable locations on the planet. The unique ecology of Antarctica revolves around these and other rare residents.

VERA DA SILVA
AMAZON RIVER DOLPHIN

"Amazon river dolphins are incredible...
They are intelligent enough to survive in
a complex ecosystem that changes
seasonally with dramatic flooding. They are
a beautiful animal. And we need to save
more beautiful things in our world."

Amazon River Dolphin

→ **Scientific Name:** *Inia geoffrensis*

→ **Range:** Amazon and Orinoco river basins of South America

→ **Population Trend:** Unknown, but concern exists due to evidence of emerging threats.

→ **IUCN Status:** The Amazon river dolphin's status was changed from Vulnerable to Data Deficient in 2008 since so little is known about threats, ecology, and population numbers over much of their range.

Vera da Silva

→ **Education:** PhD from Cambridge University, United Kingdom

→ **Nationality:** Brazilian

→ **Organizational Affiliation:** Instituto Nacional de Pesquisas da Amazonia (National Institute of Amazonian Research) in Manaus, Brazil

→ **Years Working with Amazon River Dolphins:** Nearly 35

→ **Books Published:** *Amazon Dolphins*

→ **Notable Accomplishments:** Stopped misguided government plans to cull Amazon river dolphins as a competitor to local fishers; responsible for amassing most of the biological and ecological knowledge of the species available today

LOCAL legend has it that Amazon river dolphins are magical; they will come ashore at night, or onto your boat, and try to enchant you—to bring you back into their world beneath the water to live with them forever. Biologist Vera da Silva was herself enchanted by these dolphins. "I came to the Amazon to study fish," she says. "I became fascinated with the Amazon river dolphin, and I have never stopped studying them since."

Amazon river dolphins are large, pink, and serpentine, with bulging, lumpy foreheads; small, functional eyes, and long snouts lined by sharp teeth. Swimming just beneath the surface of the world's second-longest river, they are more like prehistoric sea creatures than most people's image of the playful modern-day dolphin. But they are true relatives of the better-known marine dolphins, and da Silva is convinced of their beauty and intelligence. And as the person who probably knows more about the species than anyone on Earth, she is the right person to gauge their value.

"These dolphins are incredible," she enthuses. "As top predators in the Amazon river system, they keep it clean by removing sick individual fish, and they keep the fish populations in balance by targeting overpopulous fish species. They are intelligent enough to survive in a complex ecosystem that changes seasonally with dramatic flooding during the wet season and severe reduction of their habitat during the dry season. They are a beautiful animal. And we need to save more beautiful things in our world."

There are three surviving species of purely freshwater dolphins; fewer than ten years ago there were four, and da Silva is determined that the enigmatic Amazon river dolphin will not follow the fate of its close relative, the recently extinct Yangtze river dolphin species.

Amazon river dolphins—also called pink dolphins, or *botos*—are only found in the Amazon and Orinoco river basins. They have a distinct appearance: large, flexible bodies; long, wide flippers; bulbous foreheads; and pointy, toothed snouts. These characteristics alone would make them readily identifiable, but additionally, some of the adults—typically males—have an even more defining

trait: a pink skin coloration that they take on as they age, ranging anywhere from a dull gray-pink to a hot, flamingo pink. It is unclear why this change in color from their original adolescent blue-gray shade happens. However, there are a number of theories, including scarring from battles with other males, and the onset of sexual maturity.

When da Silva first came to the Amazon in the late 1970s, almost nothing was known about Amazon river dolphins. "I came to study fish. But there was a proposal by some fishery agencies to cull the dolphins because they were thought to be overly abundant and eating too many of the same fish that the local fishermen targeted. So I decided to study the dolphin instead and see if it was true." What da Silva found was that Amazon river dolphins ate a tremendous variety of fish, and were therefore not in direct competition with local fishermen. As a result, the cull was canceled.

da Silva's work not only changed the government plans for killing dolphins, but it also put a new, more favorable light on the species. da Silva realized, though, that if the right conservation decisions were to be made for the dolphins, people would need to learn much more about their basic ecology and biology.

"I was a young widow with two small daughters that I was raising alone," she recalls. "But someone had to learn more about the species in order for decision makers to start making the right choices. The plan to cull them, based on misinformation, made this clear. So despite the long distances and weeks in the field away from

everyone, I continued to study the animal and learn everything I could." As a result, most of what is known about Amazon river dolphins is either from da Silva's and her collaborators' work, or the work of her students, whom she instructs in their research.

da Silva and her students have been studying the Amazon river dolphins in the Mamirauá Sustainable Development Reserve region in the central Amazon Rainforest. Because the forests are flooded for half the year, the region becomes an inland sea flanked by the Amazon and a large tributary, making the research particularly difficult. Despite this, da Silva has tagged more than five hundred dolphins, resulting in the first population abundance assessment for the species. Nonetheless, this is just one relatively small area within the wide distribution of the Amazon river dolphin, and the species remains unstudied in most of its range.

Outside of occasional conflict with the fishing community, the Amazon river dolphin has been mostly left alone in the past, due in part to the local folklore attributing magical powers to the

What You Should Know about Amazon River Dolphins

→ Amazon river dolphins are born bluish gray and frequently lighten with age to a pink color, most prominently in males.

→ Males collect and display items in the water, such as seaweed, wood, or rocks, to attract the attention of female Amazon river dolphins.

→ In studied populations, females and their young retreated into the deep forests during flooding season while males stayed in the vicinity of main river channels and lakes.

→ Amazon river dolphins have only been successfully bred in one zoological facility in the world, located in Venezuela.

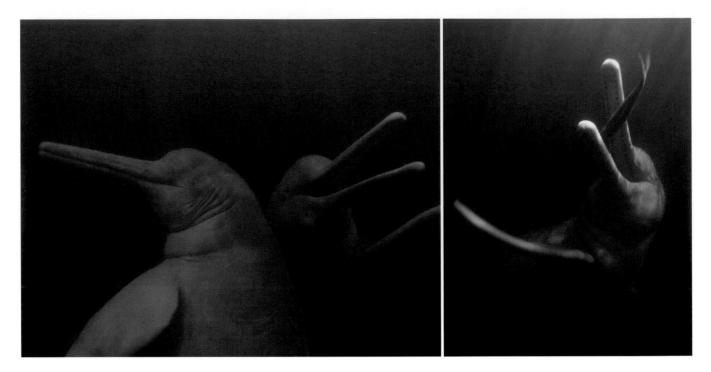

species. Unfortunately, outside influences have caused this respect to erode, and dolphins are now being killed in large numbers, chopped up, and used as bait to catch an Amazonian catfish considered commercially valuable in Colombia and today also sold in Brazilian markets.

"About a decade ago," says da Silva, "we started seeing evidence of Amazon river dolphins being brutally killed for the first time. Ten percent of the population of dolphins in my study area have disappeared, and it is because of this illegal hunting. All along we have faced the threat to their habitat from planned hydroelectric dams, and overfishing. Now we have this new threat that we must combat."

In response to these killings, da Silva has launched an awareness and education campaign, reaching out to local law enforcement, national decision makers, media, and the public. And she

has already seen progress. "Before they would hunt the dolphins in the open. Now everyone knows it is illegal. They have started killing them in secret. The next step will be to put an end to that as well."

The other two living river dolphin species that exclusively inhabit freshwater, are the Ganges and Indus river dolphins of central Southern Asia. Additionally there are a number of dolphins that can be found in both marine and freshwater systems: The small Tucuxi overlaps in habitat with the Amazon river dolphin; Irrawaddy dolphins are found in freshwater lakes and rivers of Southeast Asia, in addition to coastal and brackish waters; and the South American La Plata river dolphin occasionally inhabits freshwater, although it is primarily found in coastal salt water. While all freshwater dolphins face an array of threats to their survival, the two Asian freshwater dolphin species in particular are under extreme threat from diminished prey, fishing nets, and riparian habitat degradation—forces that led to the recent extinction of the fourth exclusively freshwater dolphin species: the Yangtze river dolphin.

Nicknamed "Goddess of the Yangtze," the Yangtze river dolphin formerly inhabited the lower and middle regions of the Yangtze River in China, along with tributaries and connected lakes. Aggressive overfishing, conflict with local fishers, and changes in habitat caused by heavy boat traffic, pollution, fishery interaction, and hydroelectric dams, led to their decline. The Yangtze river dolphin was declared functionally extinct in December 2006 when scientists were unable to find a single member of the species after a lengthy search. The announcement occurred two years after the last confirmed sighting of an individual Yangtze river dolphin was documented, and marked the first known whale or dolphin extinction in more than fifty years.

In addition to conducting and organizing river dolphin research at the National Institute of Amazonian Research in Manaus, Brazil, da Silva runs their Amazon manatee rescue and rehabilitation program. Amazonian manatees—a species considered vulnerable to extinction—are still hunted by poachers for food in the region, frequently leaving manatee young behind to die. da Silva and her colleagues rescue the orphans and raise them until they can be released back into the wild.

da Silva still spends the majority of her time, though, researching and conserving Amazon river dolphins. They "are facing the same threats that the Yangtze river dolphin faced—we are repeating these mistakes," she warns. "There are many sensitive animals and many callous people in the world. We can't be careless with this beautiful and intelligent species. We need to be smart enough to save Amazon river dolphins. I am determined we will be."

Why It Is Important to Save Amazon River Dolphins

As a top predator in the Amazon river ecosystem, these freshwater dolphins keep fish populations healthy by catching slow individuals that may have parasites or diseases, and keep certain fish populations in check so they do not overpopulate and disrupt the river system's ecological balance.

KAREN ECKERT
SEA TURTLES

"Sea turtles are now threatened at every life stage, and our conservation efforts must be intelligent and persistent."

Sea Turtles

→ **Species:** There are seven species of sea turtles worldwide.

→ **Range:** Sea turtles are found in all warm and temperate ocean waters around the globe, and some even venture into subarctic zones.

→ **Population Trend:** Six sea turtle species are well documented to be severely depleted over the coarse of the 20th century. In the case of the seventh species, the Australian flatback turtle, data are insufficient to make a determination.

→ **IUCN Status:** Three species (hawksbill, *Eretmochelys imbricata*; leatherback, *Dermochelys coriacea*; and Kemp's ridley, *Lepidochelys kempii*) are Critically Endangered. The loggerhead (*Caretta caretta*) and the green turtle (*Chelonia mydas*) are classified as Endangered. The most populous species, the olive ridley (*Lepidochelys olivacea*) is classified as Vulnerable.

Karen Eckert

→ **Education:** PhD from the University of Georgia

→ **Nationality:** American

→ **Organizational Affiliation:** Wider Caribbean Sea Turtle Conservation Network (WIDECAST)

→ **Years Working with Sea Turtles:** 30+

→ **Honors:** Chevron-Texaco Conservation Award recipient (2003); Pew fellow in Marine Conservation (1996); Inducted into the United Nations Global 500 Roll of Honour for Environmental Achievement (1994)

→ **Books Published:** Dozens, including *Sea Turtles: An Ecological Guide* and *Turning the Tide: Exploitation, Trade and Management of Marine Turtles in the Lesser Antilles, Central America, Colombia and Venezuela.*

→ **Notable Accomplishments:** Built a network of sea turtle specialists in 43 Caribbean nations and territories to coordinate and cooperate on research and conservation initiatives; authored or facilitated sea turtle action recovery plans for numerous Caribbean governments; provided the world with a successful model of multilateral marine resource management.

AFTER more than three decades, Karen Eckert still becomes animated when speaking about sea turtles. This enthusiasm and deep-felt concern are perhaps surprising, as Eckert began her academic career studying freshwater ecology in Illinois, far from any ocean. "I had never heard of a sea turtle before taking a job after college as codirector, with my husband, of the Little Cumberland Island Loggerhead Sea Turtle Research Project in Georgia. After watching huge females lumber from the sea and dig their nests, and then seeing the little hatchlings run for the water two months later, Scott and I fell in love with these gentle creatures, and with how much there was to learn and contribute. We've both stayed in the field ever since!"

Eckert is now recognized as an authority on not only the turtles themselves, but on interna-

tional conservation policy and community empowerment. Eckert serves as executive director of the Wider Caribbean Sea Turtle Conservation Network, or WIDECAST, an expert network affiliated with the United Nations' Caribbean Environment Programme. WIDECAST is tasked with preventing the extinction of all six imperiled sea turtle species found in the Caribbean basin and is one of the most active biodiversity networks in the world, encompassing forty-three nations and territories. Karen has been recognized many times, including her induction into the United Nations' Global 500 Roll of Honour for Environmental Achievement in 1994, for her efforts to develop and coordinate the network's activities.

There are seven sea turtle species, and all but two are classified as Endangered (the olive ridley was recently moved to Vulnerable, and the Australian flatback is classified as Data Deficient). Despite the shared moniker "sea turtle," there are many differences between species. Leatherback sea turtles are the largest reptiles on Earth, capable of exceeding seven feet in length and weighing more than two thousand pounds. In contrast, the diminutive ridley turtles rarely tip the scales at more than one hundred pounds.

Different sea turtles thrive on different foods. Green turtles are the only herbivorous species as adults; they have serrated jaws adapted to grazing sea grass and algae. Hawksbills have relatively narrow heads and a distinct "overbite," adapted for reaching into crevices in coral reefs for, mainly, sponges. Loggerheads and ridleys are omnivores, consuming everything from fish and crustaceans to jellyfish and seaweed. Leatherbacks typically forage on the high seas and prefer to consume jellyfish.

There are other differences, as well. For example, olive and Kemp's ridleys gather in large groups off of preferred nesting beaches where the females come ashore en masse to

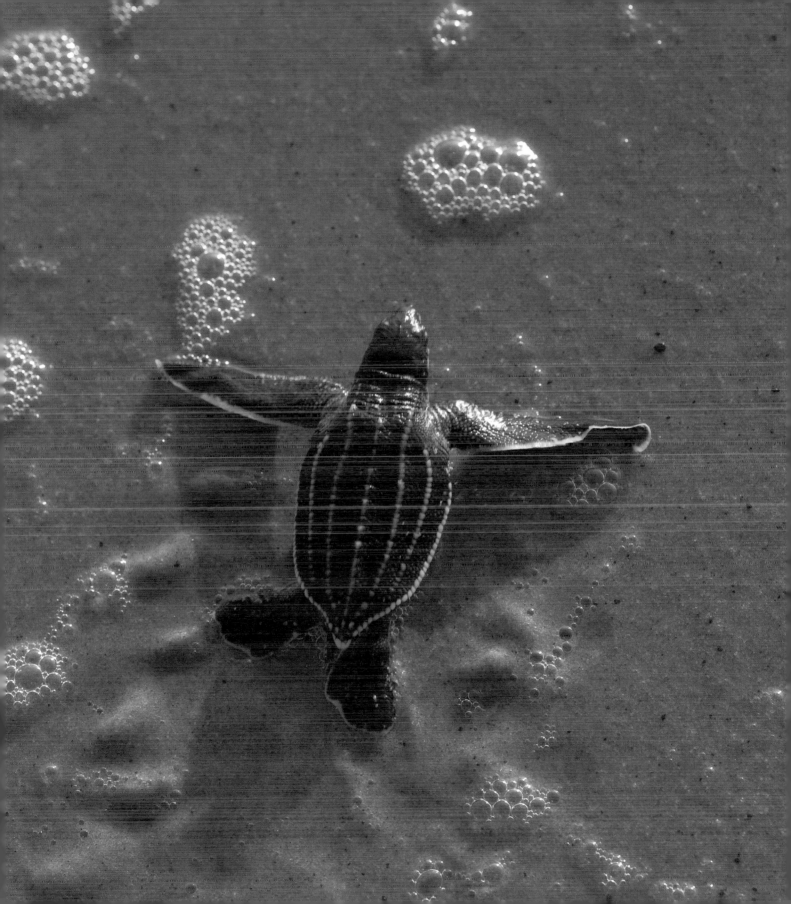

write a variety of publications that provide information on best practices for sea turtle research and management, conservation and recovery planning, education, and threat reduction. "Sharing information is a key to sea turtle survival," she says. When something works in one area, it's worth exploring in others—many countries struggle with similar conservation and management issues."

Despite ecological differences between species, sea turtles share many contemporary threats, all of which spell trouble for depleted populations. Egg-laying success is affected by loss of nesting habitat due to coastal development and pollution. Populations are reduced by the accidental catch and drowning of turtles in nets and on fishing lines (termed *bycatch*). Widespread poaching of eggs combined with natural predation effectively eliminates nesting success in some areas. And the disorientation of hatchlings due to artificial beachfront lighting, coupled with a general lack of opportunity for rural coastal people still relying on a sea turtle harvest, also hinder the recovery of depleted and declining populations.

Eckert is helping every way she knows how. "For the future of the sea turtle, we need to take all possible and practical action," she insists. "Adding to existing threats which have driven sea turtle numbers down 80 percent or more in some regions, we now have the added pressure of climate change. Small changes in the temperature of beach sand can change the gender ratio in a clutch

collectively deposit enormous numbers of eggs. The phenomenon is known as an *arribada*, which means "arrival" in Spanish. There are accounts of five hundred thousand or more females all coming ashore to lay their eggs in synchrony, which, by overwhelming local predators, may help increase the survival of offspring. Unfortunately, the numbers of females arriving to nest at many of these sites are drastically reduced from a generation ago.

To increase public awareness of the sea turtles' plight, Eckert and a colleague, David Gulko, wrote a comprehensive book called *Sea Turtles: An Ecological Guide*. Eckert has also collaborated with dozens of other experts to compile, edit, or of eggs, but, perhaps more importantly, large-scale shifts in patterns of ocean productivity may dramatically affect the distribution of food resources. Sea turtles are now threatened at every life stage, and our conservation efforts must be intelligent and persistent." Eckert also points out the necessity to take into account that long-term turtle conservation relies on achieving a higher standard of living among rural coastal inhabitants in tropical countries.

Both Eckert and her husband, Scott, are devoted to making a difference in sea turtle conservation worldwide by educating and involving local communities as a core aspect of their efforts to save these ancient species. Eckert collaborates with WIDECAST country coordinators and local scientists, community leaders, and governments in more than three dozen countries to develop comprehensive sea turtle recovery action plans. These strategies, as well as the research and management plans that result from them, are implemented with the help of WIDECAST experts and partners. Today, the Caribbean Sea is the only region on Earth where major populations of all six species of locally occurring sea turtle are rising. States Eckert, "More than 70 percent of Caribbean governments protect sea turtles year-round now!"

For a girl from the Midwest who doesn't much care for scuba diving, Eckert has certainly made a huge impact in the water. "When I listen to Caribbean elders sharing their stories of concern over dramatic declines in Caribbean biodiversity since the days of their youth, sometimes I wonder what the future will hold. But at the same time I am inspired by young people volunteering to safeguard egg-laying females from poachers, designing outreach programs for local schools, and pursuing graduate training in marine science, and this gives me great hope that sea turtles will endure," says Eckert. "The world would certainly be a lesser place without them."

Why It Is Important to Save Sea Turtles

Females lay thousands of eggs each year along stretches of sandy coastline—those eggs that do not hatch provide nutrients to dune vegetation, which in turn prevents erosion of beach habitats. Eggs and hatchlings are an important food source for numerous bird, fish, crustacean, reptile, and mammalian predators. Sea turtles also help to maintain ecological balance in coral reefs and sea grass, which in turn underpin the fisheries and tourism industries that sustain coastal economies.

AMANDA VINCENT
SEAHORSES

"There is so much more to seahorses than just the fabulous 'male pregnancy'... They are distinctive from head to tail... They are just magical little beasties."

FAST FACTS

Seahorses

→ **Species:** There are approximately 48 species of sea-horses.

→ **Range:** Shallow temperate or tropical ocean coastal waters, or in brackish waters

→ **Population Trend:** Complex seahorse ecology and behavior, coupled with significant ongoing exploitation and habitat loss, means that many populations are declining.

→ **IUCN Status:** Individual species' statuses vary between Data Deficient and Endangered.

Amanda Vincent

→ **Education:** PhD from the University of Cambridge, United Kingdom

→ **Nationality:** Canadian and British

→ **Organizational Affiliation:** Project Seahorse; University of British Columbia's Fisheries Centre

→ **Years Working with Seahorses:** 26

→ **Honors:** Finalist, Indianapolis Prize (2010); Chevron Conservation Award (2006); Pew Fellowship in Marine Conservation (2000); named Leader for the 21st Century by *Time* magazine (1999); Rolex Award for Enterprise (1998); Grand Prix International pour l'Environment Marin (1998); Whitley Award in Animal Conservation, Royal Geographical Society (1994)

→ **Publications:** Coauthored *Seahorses: An Identification Guide to the World's Species and Their Conservation*

→ **Notable Accomplishments:** First scientist to study sea-horses underwater and first to uncover global trade in seahorses; Project Seahorse is the IUCN Red List authority for the seahorse family

"IT'S shocking how many people don't realize that seahorses are fish," says seahorse expert Amanda Vincent. "Seahorses are thought of as something special, while most fish are just thought of as food. This benefits the seahorses by garnering public interest in their survival, but it also works against them when it comes to the wildlife trade, which 'markets' species and their unique qualities." Seahorses, which can be found in shallow tropical and temperate waters around all continents except Antarctica, are currently heavily collected for use in aquarium display and in traditional Asian medicines.

Vincent's road to becoming the world's foremost specialist and conservationist for seahorses, and their close relatives sea dragons and pipefish, actually started with a trip to find out more about herself. Although she had traveled extensively with her family growing up, after graduating from college, she decided to take time off and

What You Should Know about Seahorses

→ Scientists disagree, but there are believed to be 48 different species of seahorses.

→ Seahorses vary in size from pygmy seahorses (less than two centimeters) to the Pacific seahorse (more than 35 centimeters).

→ Seahorses use camouflage for defense from predators by changing color to match their environment.

→ Male seahorses carry the embryos and give birth. Young seahorses leave their father's pouch fully formed and independent, looking like miniature adult seahorses.

Why It Is Important to Save Seahorses

Seahorses' unique reproductive behaviors could offer valuable insight into reproductive ecology. Additionally, seahorses are predator fish that prey on bottom-dwelling organisms—removal of the species from their habitat could disrupt the ecosystem balance.

experience more of the world on her own. She traveled Europe, the Middle East, Asia, and Oceania, taking seemingly random jobs, such as making wine in France, working on a kibbutz in Israel, sheep shearing in the Australian Outback, and researching dugongs (sea cows) along the coast Down Under. For two years she accumulated these experiences and then went back to a scholarship she had put on hold at Cambridge University in the United Kingdom.

"Everyone should get out of academia and experience other cultures if their goal is to make a difference in the world," she says. "After I completed my travels, I knew I wanted to help secure a future for the oceans, and develop my brain as well. That's what led me to working on seahorses and studying their reproductive biology. And the rest of my life I've been using what I learned—and continue to learn—in my travels to build on the success of what I do: first in studying seahorses, and then later in my career advocating to conserve them, which has become the thrust of my life's work."

When Vincent first started studying seahorses, very little was known about them—primarily that their reproductive habits (most notably, male "pregnancy") were intriguing. With no previous natural seahorse studies to draw from, Vincent decided to launch the first open-water study of seahorses off the coast of Florida.

"It was a disaster. I had announced to everyone I was going to go study seahorses, and when I got in the water, I couldn't find the blessed little animals!" Seahorses have evolved to perfectly blend into the underwater habitats with textured eco-skeletons and chameleon color-changing tactics that allow them to mimic their seabed surroundings. Frustrated, Vincent returned to Cambridge and tried to study them in an aquarium setting. Unfortunately, seahorses are difficult to maintain in a captive environment, and she struggled to keep her subjects alive.

After facing the frustrations of aquarium research, she decided to return to the ocean. "Sometimes you just have to plunge right in and make mistakes. Science and conservation are all about trying different things to see what works, adjusting course and learning, then trying all over again. So I went back into the water." By the end of the study, she had developed a system. "I look for the tails. The rest of the animal may be perfectly camouflaged, but it's hard to hide their tiny tails curled around a piece of sea grass or seaweed." Soon she was identifying individuals and discovering never-before-known secrets about the biology and ecology of these cryptic fishes.

Seahorses form the genus *Hippocampus*, from a combination of the Greek words for *horse* and *sea monster*, and are members of the family Syngnathidae, along with pipehorses, pipefish, and sea dragons, which includes three hundred species, forty-eight of which are seahorse species. They are best known for their unique reproductive behavior; the male gets "pregnant" when the female deposits her eggs in the male's pouch, where he fertilizes them, then carries them through their early development. His pouch acts like a womb, providing oxygen and nutrition. But Vincent discovered scores of other behaviors and biological traits outside of this special reproductive habit that made her want to keep studying the species.

"There is so much more to seahorses than just the fabulous male 'pregnancy'— they form pair bonds, with courtship rituals every morning. They are so faithful that when one is injured, the other will forgo mating opportunities until its mate heals. They

are distinctive from head to tail, and there are thousands of ways they are amazing: They can change colors rapidly; they have no stomach or teeth but are great predators; and they have a prehensile tail that makes them the only fish that can 'hold hands'!"

Unfortunately, seahorses are threatened by a number of pressures—in particular, trade for traditional Asian medicines, aquarium collections, and as souvenirs and curios. They also suffer from habitat loss, and are a bycatch victim from shrimp trawling nets and other commercial fishing operations that occur in their habitat.

Vincent cofounded Project Seahorse in 1996 to develop projects tackling all the different needs for seahorse conservation, and in 2002 she was able to further her Project Seahorse work through her new role as Canada research chair in marine conservation at the University of British Columbia's Fisheries Centre. Like Vincent's career, Project Seahorse also evolved and expanded its scope. Early on, its accomplishments were primarily in accumulating base knowledge of seahorses through painstaking research; Vincent herself logged more than a thousand hours observing seahorses underwater for her doctoral thesis. Later successes include community outreach efforts in Southeast Asia, such as creating alliances of small-scale fishers who now work closely with provincial governments for better fishing regulation enforcement, and working with the traditional Asian medicine communities in Asia and North America to promote sustainable practices. Project Seahorse also monitors global trade in seahorses, developing extensive

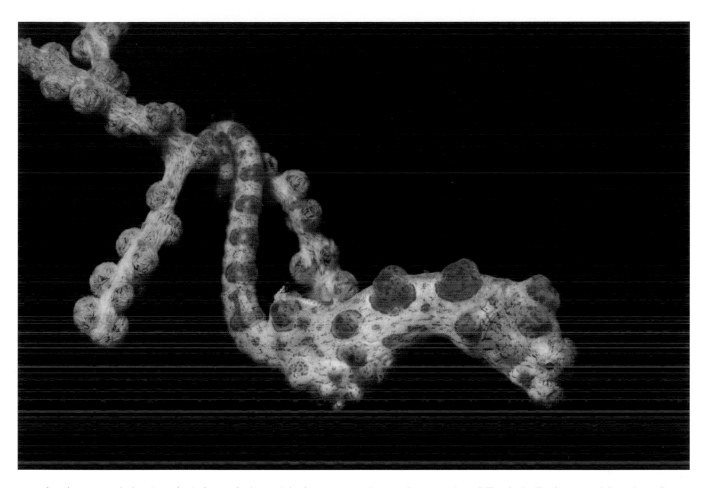

databases and sharing their knowledge with the public, media, and decision makers. Project Seahorse policy initiatives have also been creative and impressive in their scope and impact, including creating marine protected areas and national legislation benefiting shallow-water species by conserving seahorse habitat in the Philippines.

Additionally, Vincent and Project Seahorse achieved a landmark international policy victory for seahorses in 2002, when as a result of a successful campaign to gain global protections for seahorses from unsustainable trade, all forty-eight species of seahorse were placed on Appendix II of the Convention on International Trade in Endangered Species of Wild Fauna and Flora, also known as CITES. This historic victory made seahorses the first marine fish genus to receive such global protection.

"The work we do at Project Seahorse—policy, research, on-the-ground campaigns—all benefits hundreds of species. But seahorses are a flagship helping us focus. If the world is a bit of an onion, I see seahorses as the green heart. They have enormous charisma, which maybe will rub off a bit on other, less-celebrated fish. Seahorses capture that connection for other marine life. They are just magical little beasties."

DAVID WILEY
GREAT WHALES

"I was out there every day on the water, observing whales hour after hour, and I got hooked. There were so many mysteries about whales, things that no one knew, and I could watch them from the boat without ever tiring of it."

FAST FACTS

Great Whales

→ **Species:** There are 13 species of great whales.

→ **Range:** Great whales are far-ranging and can be found in most the world's oceans, including the polar extremes.

→ **Population Trends:** Vary by species and individual populations, with many population trends unknown. Some populations of whales, such as humpbacks, southern rights, and gray whales, are thought to be expanding.

→ **IUCN Status:** Of the thirteen great whales, one is Vulnerable, five are Endangered, and two are Data Deficient.

David Wiley

→ **Education:** PhD from Antioch University, New England

→ **Nationality:** American

→ **Organizational Affiliation:** National Oceanic and Atmospheric Administration

→ **Years Working with Whales:** 20+

→ **Honors:** Recipient of Fullbright's Ian Axford Fellowship (2010); U.S. Commerce Department's Individual Gold Medal (2009); Alumni Environmental Excellence Award, Antioch University New England (2008); National Oceanic and Atmospheric Administration (NOAA) Employee of the Year Award (2007); Massachusetts Society for the Prevention of Cruelty to Animals' Human Hero Award (2007); Switzer Foundation Environmental Leadership Award (2001); Gulf of Maine/Bay of Fundy Visionary Award (1993)

→ **Notable Accomplishments:** Lead author of paper that scientifically documented for the first time that marine mammal stranding victims were successfully surviving rescue and return efforts; pioneered advances in whale-friendlier fishing gear; led the science and advocacy efforts resulting in moving shipping lanes out of heavily trafficked North Atlantic right whale migration routes

WORKING to save whales was never on David Wiley's radar screen growing up. Having lived his early life in upstate New York, he never even saw an ocean until he moved to the Massachusetts coast for a teaching job when he was twenty-four. But after determining that an indoor job was not the right personal fit, he decided to embrace his love of nature and took a position as a naturalist on a whale-watching boat. "I had never had the intention of studying whales," he said. "But I was out there every day on the water, observing whales hour after hour, and I got hooked. There were so many mysteries about whales, things that no one knew, and I could watch them from the boat without ever tiring of it."

Off the coast of Massachusetts where Wiley worked, he could see humpback, fin, minke, pilot, and right whales, as well as rare, occasional spottings of other whales, such as sperm, beluga, and blue whales. "Working on the whale-watching boat provided me with thousands of hours of observation," he says, "a luxury most researchers don't have. I learned to appreciate the whales I watched as individuals, and that has played a role in reinforcing my commitment to protecting them, as well as informing my conservation and research efforts."

Whales are found in all the world's oceans, including the polar extremes. The subset of whales known as the "great whales" includes the sperm whale, the largest toothed whale, and twelve species of baleen whales. Baleen, sometimes referred to as *whalebone*—a misnomer, as it is not bone at all—is a food-filtering device made of the protein keratin, allowing baleen whales to take in and expel large amounts of seawater while ingesting their targeted catch, such as small fish, krill, and copepods.

In 1989 Wiley took a job as a conservation scientist for the International Wildlife Coalition. In that role, Wiley was the lead author on a groundbreaking paper that changed the way many scientists and academics viewed marine mammal strandings. "Up until that time," he says, "the scientific community typically wrote off mass stranded whales and dolphins as a lost cause. There were committed organizations and individuals working to save and rehabilitate stranded animals, but the general consensus of the scientific community was that these stranded animals were doomed to die on the shore, or re-strand if an attempt was made to put them back into the water—euthanasia was seen as the only responsible course of action by most scientists. I did not see any data that really supported the euthanasia position and wanted to challenge that dogma." Working with the Cape Cod Stranding Network, Wiley set up a scientifically rigorous experiment in which they recorded, treated, tagged, and rereleased seventy-seven different stranded pilot whales, white-sided dolphins, and common dolphins, then tracked their survival. What they found was that most of the rescued cetaceans from these mass strandings not only survived the transport to the release area, but they did not re-strand themselves and appeared to be successful in returning to the wild. "We forced the scientific community to rethink all of their assumptions about mass strandings; they were no longer able to dismiss important stranding work as fruitless, and this has resulted in more funding and more support for the stranding efforts than had been happening up to that point."

Wiley eventually went back to school and got his doctorate in environmental studies, then returned to the Cape to work as a research coordinator at the Stellwagen Bank National Marine Sanctuary. In his new position, Wiley was able to analyze the many threats affecting the whales at the sanctuary, and start thinking about solutions.

The treks of migratory whales, which base their migration routes on essential feeding, mating, and calf-rearing requirements, can bring them into conflict with fishing and ocean vessels, threats that continue to take their toll on some of the rarest of whale species. "I had worked on designing whale-friendlier fishing gear as part of my PhD," says Wiley, "and we knew the whales at the sanctuary were being caught up in fishing and lobster gear, resulting in injuries and mortality, so I decided to start there. The question was, what could be done about the

problem that would allow the fishermen to continue earning their livelihoods, but would at the same time protect the whales? As a multiple-use marine sanctuary, we always had to keep that balance in mind."

Wiley started testing breakaway links for fishing gear that would allow whales to escape after entanglement. By testing placement and strength requirements for links in both gillnet gear and lobster gear, he was able to pioneer the technique as a possible tool for saving whales within the Stellwagen sanctuary's borders and beyond. "It seemed like this would work, but there was resistance from some of the fishermen and lobstermen. They weren't even convinced that their gear was a real problem."

To demonstrate the need for new approaches to the current fishing practices in the sanctuary, Wiley began tagging North Atlantic right whales and humpback whales to see how they were using their ocean habitat—from top to bottom. What he saw confirmed that the whales were swimming right along the floor of the sanctuary where the fishing gear was being placed. By partnering with the University of New Hampshire, he was able to use data visualization techniques combining tag data with information about the topography, and create a video showing the concurrent behavior of whales and fishing gear placement. When fishing crews saw the video, they were able to see first-hand the threat their gear posed to whales, and were more willing to work with Wiley and his colleagues and fish in ways that might be less harmful to whales.

Wiley's next work challenge was addressing whale mortalities from ship strikes in the sanctuary. Critically endangered North Atlantic right whales in particular are vulnerable to collisions with the ships going through the sanctuary and other areas, so Wiley wanted to do something about it.

Once thought to be plentiful, the North Atlantic right whales were nearly driven to extinction by commercial whaling. Today there are only a few hundred of these whales left along the North American coast, rendering the population extremely vulnerable to extinction; even occasional losses to ship strikes or fishing gear entanglement could be enough to push the species over the brink.

To address the threat from ship strikes in the Cape Cod region, Wiley spent six months working with the Boston shipping community, together poring over the whale observation data he and his colleagues had amassed in the sanctuary. After considerable negotiation and testing of ideas and information, Wiley came up with a plan for shifting the navigation lanes used by shippers transiting the sanctuary that would move them from high-use whale areas to low-use areas. Because they were part of the process, the shippers supported the change and voluntarily used the new lanes. Wiley's efforts resulted in a significant reduction in threat to whales in the sanctuary, as well as a reduction in threat to the critically endangered North Atlantic right whale from ship strikes. Using Wiley's model, shipping lanes have now been changed in other hot spots for right whales, as well as for humpbacks and fins, and coupled with recent laws requiring ships to slow down when there is a higher likelihood of collisions, prospects for the recovery of the North Atlantic right whale have significantly improved.

"There are still many threats out there to the great whales that need to be addressed—noise pollution from shipping, climate change, and of course, the unknowns about continued commercial whaling, and we need to keep testing, expanding, and improving the advancements made on ship strike and entanglement problems. The answers are out there. And people truly care about whales. So if all the different stakeholders can keep working together, we can make the oceans safer for the Great Whales. And that is what everybody ultimately wants for these spectacular animals."

Why It Is Important to Save the Great Whales

The great whales are top-feeders in their ecosystems, controlling the populations of other creatures in their habitat by consuming massive amounts of species such as krill, copepods, plankton, and small fish every day. Additionally, whale watching generates more than $2 billion annually for coastal areas in more than 100 countries.

DIANE MCTURK
GIANT RIVER OTTER

"I'll take in all otters that come my way; I'll care for them as my children until they are ready to begin their own lives on the river. And I'll protect the river and wetlands so they can thrive once again."

Giant River Otter

→ **Scientific Name:** *Pteronura brasiliensis*

→ **Range:** The historic range extended throughout rivers and streams in northern and central South America. Now 80 percent of its range has disappeared.

→ **Population Trend:** Declining. It is estimated just 1,000 to 5,000 giant otters remain.

→ **IUCN Status:** Endangered

Diane McTurk

→ **Nationality:** Guyanese

→ **Organizational Affiliation:** Karanambu Trust, and Karanambu Lodge Inc.

→ **Years Working with Giant River Otters:** 30+

→ **Honors:** Guyana Tourism Authority's "Tourism Pioneer" Award (2010); Tourism & Hospitality Award for Excellence in Conservation (1999); Medal of Service from the president of Guyana, Cheddi Jagan (1996)

→ **Notable Accomplishments:** Has raised more than 45 orphaned giant river otters; founder and current executive director of the Karanambu Trust; secretary of Karanambu Lodge, Inc.

MOST would figure that a species that spends a majority of its life in or near the water would be born natural swimmers, but giant otter babies need to be taught to swim. And if your chosen passion involves rescuing orphaned otters, as it does for Diane McTurk, this is a significant challenge. But this is just one of the adversities McTurk must address when she cares for, raises, and protects the giant river otters of southern Guyana. "I was given my first orphan otter back in 1985," she says. "Since then I've raised more than forty-five youngsters and released them all back to the wild. Sometimes they return to visit, and they bring their entire families with them!"

Rescue and rehabilitation is just one aspect of McTurk's passion. Preserving the traditional Amerindian (indigenous people of the Americas) lifestyle of the North Rupununi is also part of her mission. "You can't just save a species. The survival of the otter is linked to the health of the entire ecosystem and all the members of the community that affect it," states McTurk. The McTurk family settled in the North Rupununi in 1927, but it was McTurk's great-great-grandfather who first immigrated to Guyana from Scotland around 1790. With this long family history, it is understandable that she feels a powerful tie to the land. Wanting to share her

family-owned paradise with others, McTurk opened an eco-lodge at their Karanambo Ranch, now known as Karanambu Lodge, where she invites guests to visit with the otters and learn about their plight. It was McTurk's work with the otters and her increasing realization that she needed to protect the ecosystem in which they thrive that led the McTurks to set up the Karanambu Trust, a charity organization dedicated to the protection and sustainable use of the wetlands in partnership with local communities.

Increasing development of the fragile habitat of the otters and other wildlife threatens the unspoiled landscape, like the Rupununi River system, which harbors more than two hundred species of mammals alone and an amazing diversity of life—including giant anteaters, arapaimas, jaguars, tapirs, macaws, ocelots, eagles, and of course, the critically endangered giant river otter.

The largest species of freshwater otter, giant river otters reach up to eighty pounds and seven feet in length. Because of the otter cubs' intelligence and natural playfulness, Amerindian fishers sometimes capture them out of the wild and take them home to their villages to keep as pets—until the cubs grow too big to handle and their desire for food increases as well. Giant otter cubs are not only very vocal when hungry; they also bite. As a result, the orphans are frequently sent to McTurk, which is how she receives the vast majority of her charges, although sometimes she receives abandoned off-spring as well. But no matter how they come in, they all want to eat. McTurk employs a full-time fisherman just to keep the otters happy and full. An adult otter can eat up to ten pounds of fish a day.

The otter's insatiable appetite for fish, especially piranha, is why they have long been considered competitors to fisher-men's livelihoods across much of South America. Giant otters

What You Should Know about Giant River Otters

→ Giant river otters are only found in the South American rivers and tributaries of the Amazon, Orinoco, and La Plata.

→ The giant river otter is among the noisiest, most vocal, and most social of otter species, with screams, whistles, snorts, barks, growls, hums, squeaks, whines, and coos often heard in otter groups.

→ Giant river otters are longer than even their large cousin the sea otter. Young grow rapidly at first, but do not reach their full size until the age of two and a half to three years.

→ They are known in Guyana and Suriname as "water dogs," and in other parts of South America as "river wolves."

are often killed just for being there, which is one reason they have a hard time increasing their population, even today. Additionally these otters, like the more densely furred Northern Hemisphere's sea otter, were once prized for their pelts. Poaching giant otters peaked in the 1950s and '60s, but the resulting decline was devastating. Fewer than five thousand are currently estimated to survive in the wild today. They are considered the most endangered mammal in the neotropics, with habitat loss the biggest continuing threat. Guyana still retains about 75 percent of its forests, but logging, oil concessions, and increasing human populations mean even less of a chance for recovery as roads, pollution, and disturbance become more prevalent along the rivers where otters live.

"I'll take in all otters that come my way; I'll care for them as my children until they are ready to begin their own lives on the river. And I'll protect the river and wetlands so they can thrive once again." McTurk provides a chance for the otters to return to where they were born and interact with wild otters that range along the Rupununi River near Karanambu. These interactions finish off the critical species "training." There is, of course, the risk that the orphans will not survive this transition back to the wild, but McTurk has always felt it best to give her beloved beasts a chance to live the same life as the other otters around this special place. If all goes well, the second-chance otters will find mates and contribute their valuable genes to a shallow pool of surviving wild otters.

So while there is a long history of persecution against giant river otters and many threats facing them still today, if there is a future for them, it may just start with a family-run eco-lodge, a local charity, and a woman in Guyana who helps teach orphaned otters how to swim.

AIR
WORKING IN THE SKY AND CANOPY

BY STEFANIE POWERS, WILDLIFE ADVOCATE
AND ACTRESS

Message from My Heart

I cannot remember a time in my life when animals were not present. First, the family pets. Then, everything that fell out of a tree or was hit by a car was brought to my mother for care and rescue. But it was growing up under the influence of my stepfather, who bred racehorses and collected exotic animals, that was the turning point in my life. He was determined to imbue me with a full understanding of the responsibilities required of people who take into their care, for benefit or for pleasure, wild or domesticated animals. To emphasize his point, he took me to the holding pens at a slaughterhouse, where we saw horses—young, old, beautiful, and ugly—all there because someone did not accept the required full responsibility. It was a tough lesson but an indelible one.

It was a natural extension to those formative years that sometime later I would rescue an eight-week-old Malaysian sun bear being sold as a curiosity. I brought the baby home with enough formula to nurse him until he could transition to fruits and proteins. Much to the surprise of my housekeeper, I installed "Eugene" in the kitchen to play with my Yorkshire terrier and my Doberman pinscher and waited to break the news to my husband.

After a stiff drink, I less than subtly broached the subject: "You like bears, don't you?" I asked an astonished face, and promptly produced our new charge. I accepted the commitment to care for him and obtained the necessary permits to have him on my property in a compound purposely built for his needs, although he spent most days up the many pine trees on the four acres of land where he roamed freely. There were many adventures and many changes of house during Eugene's twelve years with me as his protector. He was a remarkable creature who was atypically gentle for his species and never lost the imprint of his infancy spent as a member of my family. These stories don't always turn out so well.

During my journey with Eugene and the countless dogs, horses, and cats I've adopted, as well as my thirty-eight-year relationship with my Amazonian yellow-naped parrot, Papuga, I have learned an enormous amount about the human-animal bond that has supported us throughout history, and I have benefited more than anything from the privilege of sharing my life with them.

Eugene opened the door to the wonderful world of wildlife for me, but it was my relationship with actor/conservationist William Holden that took me to East Africa, where, unbeknownst to me at the time, I would make a lifelong commitment to wildlife conservation and the protection of flora and fauna.

Bill was a conservationist long before the word was in our popular vocabulary. At the beginning of the 1960s, he and two partners established the first game ranch in East Africa, the purpose of which was the breeding and protection of thirty-seven species whose future existence would become so threatened that some would only be visible in zoos. After Bill's death in 1981, I established the William Holden Wildlife Foundation with the help of his two partners in Kenya. The idea was to back up the ongoing preservation work of the game ranch, (now a wildlife conservancy) with an education program for locals. Currently our center serves eleven thousand students per year and has an outreach component that extends itself to rural population centers through primary and secondary schools.

In between the activities of my acting career, I have devoted years earning my stripes in the field and on the frontlines. I created the Jaguar Conservation Trust for Jaguar Cars Ltd., which set a groundbreaking precedent in the automotive world by being the first car manufacturer to dedicate itself to the preservation of the species it uses as its name and logo. I have operated the JCT for five years, giving small grants to grassroots conservation work done by indigenous people in Belize, Guatemala, and Costa Rica. I am a dedicated activist for the preservation and protection of the American wild horse, and I have served on the boards and advisory boards of three zoos in the United States and the species survival program of the East African bongo.

I salute my many colleagues who are wildlife warriors in the battle to preserve what we are losing at an alarming rate, and I ask you, the reader, one question: If all the species of flora and fauna that make our world unique in our solar system contribute to our environment, what is our role if not as caretakers?

Steel, cement, and glass cannot replace jungles, trees, and shrubs. Our planet is a living, breathing thing, rapidly disappearing in front of our very eyes. How can we unite our neighborhoods, cities, states, and countries to join the fight to resuscitate our spaceship . . . *Planet Earth?* The heroes celebrated in this book will help us gain a greater understanding and appreciation for what it takes.

ALISON JOLLY

LEMURS

"If there's anything I've learned and tried to share, it's that everything is connected. You can't save lemurs without saving people."

Alison Jolly

→ **Education:** PhD from Yale

→ **Nationality:** American

→ **Organizational Affiliation:** Sussex University, United Kingdom

→ **Years Working with Lemurs:** 50

→ **Honors:** Knighthood of National Order of Madagascar; lifetime achievement award, International Primatological Society (2010); A new species of mouse lemur (Microcebus jollyae) was named in her honor (2006)

→ **Books Published:** *Lucy's Legacy: Sex and Intelligence in Human Evolution*; *Lords and Lemurs: Mad Scientists, Kings with Spears, and Diversity in Madagascar*; *Ring-tailed Lemur Biology: Lemur catta in Madagascar*; *A World Like Our Own: Man and Nature in Madagascar*; *The Evolution of Primate Behavior*; and children's books *Ako the Aye-Aye*; *Bitika the Mouse Lemur*; *Tik-Tik the Ringtailed Lemur*; *Bounce the White Sifaka*; and *Furry and Fuzzy the Red Ruffed Lemur Twins*

→ **Notable Accomplishments:** A pioneer in the study of primate behavior; one of the first scientists to study lemurs in the wild

Lemurs

→ **Species:** Lemurs belong to the infraorder Lemuriformes. There is scientific disagreement as to the status of species versus subspecies, with numbers of species ranging from 50 to 101 if you count all subspecies as well.

→ **Range:** All lemurs are found in just one location—the island of Madagascar.

→ **Population Trend:** Declining, due to habitat degradation, clearing of land for agriculture, and hunting

→ **IUCN Status:** Eight species are listed as Critically Endangered, eighteen are Endangered, fifteen are listed as Vulnerable, and four are Near Threatened.

ACCORDING to Alison Jolly, it was luck that led her to a career in wildlife conservation and observation that has spanned six decades. Jolly began studying lemurs back in 1963 and hasn't stopped since. She was actually studying sponges when Dr. John Buettner-Janusch arrived from Madagascar with the first large collection of prosimians, or primitive primates, ever seen in America. Jolly relates, "Even as a grad student at Yale, I still hadn't figured out exactly what I wanted to focus on until the lemurs showed up. From that moment on, there was too much to discover to stop working with them!"

The lemurs were later moved and became part of the famous primate research center at Duke University. The Duke Lemur Center currently has a successful breeding and educational program and regularly houses over 250 endangered lemurs for study to gain a better understanding of their behavior

What You Should Know about Lemurs

→ Most lemurs have four to six lower front teeth, evenly spaced close together for use in grooming—called a *toothcomb*.

→ Many lemur species are social, often living in groups or sharing sleeping spaces. Atypical in primates, females are the dominant sex.

→ The many different species of lemurs consume a wide variety of food, including fruits, plants, insects, and even small vertebrates.

→ Since humans arrived on Madagascar fewer than 1,000 years ago, at least 16 lemur species have gone extinct, including one roughly the size of a gorilla.

→ Lemurs are important in Madagascar folklore, which has resulted in some lemurs being protected against persecution with cultural taboos, while others are targeted because of superstitions requiring that they be killed on sight.

and also help conserve the biodiversity of Madagascar. These happen to be the central themes of Jolly's work as well. "I love Madagascar, and not only because of the lemurs. Some local people are strong advocates for their unique fauna—but they have so many challenges, from poverty to climate change. If there's anything I've learned and tried to share, it's that everything is connected. You can't save the lemurs without involving the people."

Jolly was one of the first scientists to study lemurs in the wild. She delved into the private life of ring-tailed lemurs on a small nature reserve in southern Madagascar, called Berenty. Jolly still travels there each spring, when all new babies are born, to follow and update her study subjects. "What most people don't understand about studying behavior is that you never know enough; the work is never complete," she says. "It only leads to more questions. What I find most fascinating is how lemurs fit very few molds we had created for primates before."

Most lemurs have a matriarchal social structure, uncommon among mammals, and even more so among primates. Lemurs are only found on the island of Madagascar—nowhere else in the world. There they fill diurnal and nocturnal, arboreal and terrestrial niches, with perhaps one hundred distinct lemur species recognized. Prior to humans settling Madagascar, gorilla-sized lemurs roamed the island. Today, lemurs range in size from the seven- to ten-kilogram (about fifteen- to twenty-two-pound) panda-colored indri to the twenty-five-gram (about one ounce) pygmy mouse lemur. Lemurs also come in a wide range of colors and characteristics, including: the black-and-white ruffed and red ruffed lemurs that resemble adorable stuffed animals; the slender Verreaux's sifakas, famous for their dancing leaps both in the trees and on the ground; dwarf lemurs, which look like their prosimian cousins called "bush babies"; and the mysterious nocturnal aye-aye, which has bat ears, beaver teeth, and a skeletally thin middle finger for probing into insect tunnels in dead trees.

Why It Is Important to Save Lemurs

All of the many varied species of lemurs can only be found on the island of Madagascar, where they have evolved to fit ecological niches throughout the island. If lemurs continue to disappear from habitat destruction and overexploitation on the island, they will cease to exist in the wild entirely.

Jolly's specialty, however, is studying the ring-tailed lemur: the most social of lemur species. It lives in southern Madagascar, in habitats ranging from high mountains to lush gallery forests to the surreal "spiny forest." Lemurs as a whole depend on smell as well as sight. Ring-tailed males challenge each other by "stink fights." A male rubs his odorous wrist glands on his tail, then shivers the tail over his back at his opponent. Between males this is clearly aggressive, but females pay close attention—and are apparently impressed.

Unfortunately, fully 80 percent of Madagascar's old-growth forest habitat has been logged or converted to agriculture. Madagascar attempted, under the leadership of former president Marc Ravalomanana, to increase protected areas for wildlife, but recent years of political upheaval have only made things worse in many areas. "It's a vicious circle," states Jolly. "The more habitat that is lost, the fewer animals you have that can fulfill the role of replanting that forest—and that's an important role. You can't have one without the other." Along with habitat loss, lemurs are also hunted for food. The vast majority of lemur species are listed as Vulnerable, Threatened, or already Endangered.

Besides Jolly's scientific contributions, her most important benefits to lemur conservation revolve around her understanding and promotion of education—both of young university scientists, and now of schoolchildren. "The people of Madagascar are wonderful. Gracious. Thoughtful. Kind. But only Malagasy people themselves can hope to save the lemurs, fossa, chameleons, and orchids of Madagas-car. To say nothing of the reefs, corals, and unique fish found off the island's coasts." Unfortunately, Madagascar is one of the economically poorest countries in the world. Its resources have been stretched beyond its limits, and many areas are extremely degraded, leaving little room for the creatures who share this unique island environment.

During more than a standard lifetime measure of contributions to science, Jolly has provided distinctive insight into the evolution of both lemur and human behavior—sex, intelligence, social life, etc. But her passion for conservation has now emerged as a children's book author, helping inspire people to care about lemurs. With her colleague, Dr. Hantanirina Rasamimanana of the university teacher's college, and renowned wildlife artist Deborah Ross, she has written six storybooks about the adventures of young lemurs, which UNICEF is disseminating through Malagasy schools. These children's books, part of the Ako Project, allow lemur enthusiasts to learn scientifically accurate information in an engaging storytelling format—a break from more traditional academic literature on lemur species.

Jolly has received many honors, including knighthood in the National Order of Madagascar, and a lifetime achievement award from her colleagues in the International Primatological Society. Best of all, to her, in 2006 a new species of tiny mouse lemur was named in her honor, *Microcebus jollyae*. Perhaps after all of Jolly's decades of effort, the little mouse lemur will survive into a future where all creatures and people on Madagascar will be given the opportunity to thrive.

MERLIN TUTTLE
BATS

"There's no better way to demonstrate how important bats are than to show them eating insect pests."

Bats

- **Species:** There are more than 1,100 species of bats in the world, all belonging to the scientific order *Chiroptera*.

- **Range:** Bats live in every habitat on Earth except for extreme desert or polar environments.

- **Population Trend:** Some bat populations are stable and number in the millions, but approximately 50 percent of the United States' bat species are in decline or already listed as Endangered. Other bat species declines are occurring worldwide.

- **IUCN Status:** Bat status trends are poorly documented. Some species have become extinct without ever having been evaluated or listed as Threatened.

Merlin Tuttle

- **Education:** PhD from the University of Kansas

- **Nationality:** American

- **Organizational Affiliation:** Bat Conservation International

- **Years Working with Bats:** 50+

- **Honors:** United Nations Environment Programme Honorary Ambassador for the Year of the Bat (2011); U.S. Congressional Award (2007); Garden Club of America Margaret Douglas Medal (2003); National Wildlife Federation's National Conservation Achievement Award (2001); Chevron Conservation Award (1997); National Fish and Wildlife Federation Chuck Yeager Award (1997); Society for Conservation Biology's Distinguished Achievement Award (1991); Gerrit S. Miller Jr. Award (1986)

- **Books Published:** *America's Neighborhood Bats: Understanding and Learning to Live in Harmony* and *The Bat House Builder's Handbook*

- **Notable Accomplishments:** Founded Bat Conservation International; *National Geographic* photographer; U.S. Postal Service featured Tuttle's photography on four stamps in 2002.

MERLIN Tuttle began questioning what people thought they knew about bats when he was just a teenager. After careful observations of gray bats in a local cave, Tuttle recognized that they probably migrated, contrary to books stating that gray bats lived in a single cave year-round. Tuttle captured the attention of leading bat experts of the time and was encouraged to take his interest in bats further—which he certainly did. Not only did he prove beyond a doubt that this species migrated, but over the next few decades, his name became synonymous with bats among those who work to study and protect them. His nickname is, most fittingly, Batman.

Though Tuttle and the few others like him that find the flying mammals fascinating, bats

Why It Is Important to Save Bats

Bats devour insects that cause damage to plants and agriculture, reducing financial loss and the need for harmful pesticides. Also, some tropical plant species depend entirely on bats for their flower pollination and seed dispersal.

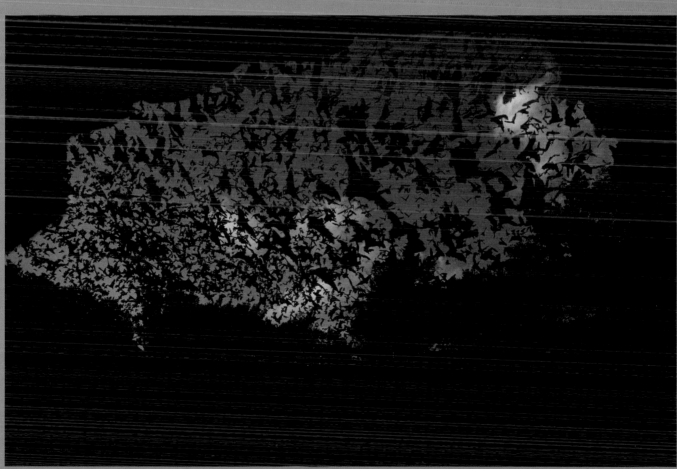

What You Should Know about Bats

→ More than two-thirds of bat species eat insects—one small pregnant or lactating female will eat her weight in insects—up to 1,000 insects in just one hour.

→ The name of their Latin scientific order, *Chiroptera*, literally means "hand wing," referring to the fact that their wings are also their arms, which in addition to flying are also used for climbing and grasping.

→ Bats are the only truly flying mammals—other so-called flying mammals, such as flying squirrels, actually glide, not fly.

→ Insect-eating bats rely on echolocation to track and catch their prey at night.

→ A bat's echolocation is far more sophisticated than any sonar humans have developed.

have virtually always had an image problem with the general public. People have worked hard to rid their land of bats. Even a farmer who allowed Tuttle to study the bat cave on his property told him, "Kill as many of them as you can while you're in there." What the farmer didn't understand at the time was how beneficial bats are. When Tuttle returned with handfuls of discarded wings from the farmer's most destructive crop pest, the potato beetle, the farmer quickly changed his mind about bats. Thanks to Tuttle, he realized he needed to preserve these bats in order to keep his crops healthy. In fact, the health of the environment depends on bats as pollinators, seed dispersers, and as insect-eating machines—an individual gray bat is estimated to eat up to three thousand or more insects a night. How bats catch that many insects in the dark is an evolutionary wonder known as *echolocation*. This sophisticated method of navigation is also what keeps them from getting tangled in human hair—many people's number one fear about bats. "It just won't happen," says Tuttle. "I've tried to tangle bats in hair, and it simply isn't possible!"

Bats represent 20 percent of mammals worldwide. A vast majority eat primarily insects; most other species consume fruits, nectar, or small animals. Just three Latin American species—commonly known as "vampire bats"—survive on the blood of mammals and birds. This rare behavior plus common misconceptions have led to their continued persecution. Tuttle feels strongly that education is a key factor in saving bats. "There's just so much misinformation out there—they are not blind, they don't attack humans, and very few species feed on blood."

Tuttle became an expert photographer in order to reveal bats in a better light. "Nearly all the photos I saw of bats showed them snarling. I wanted to show how cool bats really are—in flight, while eating, even while capturing insects. And there's no better way to demonstrate how important bats are than to show them eating insect pests." To make sure the correct information is available to bat lovers and haters alike, Tuttle has authored several bat books, among them *America's Neighborhood Bats: Understanding and Learning to Live in Harmony* and *The Bat House Builder's Handbook*. He also founded the organization Bat Conservation International (BCI) to address not only the reputation of bats, but the protection of these important species. One of the organization's first big conservation successes was in Austin, Texas, where Tuttle moved BCI's center of operations due to an increasingly fearful populace concerned about bats roosting under a newly remodeled downtown bridge. Residents were demanding the extermination of thousands of "invading bats." Tuttle spent months educating, explaining, and politicking for the bats. It worked. Today Austin generates millions of dollars in local revenue from visitors who come to see the spectacle of 1.5 million bats emerging from their daytime roost each summer evening.

Tuttle has worked in every major bat eco-region, studying and learning about bats. And with more than eleven hundred different species of bats found everywhere except the most extreme polar and desert habitats, this has kept him enthralled and very busy. But bats are now facing a new and deadly threat, white-nose syndrome. Entire colonies of bats, hundreds of thousands at a time, are wiped out by this disease each winter, with reported mortality rates

approaching 100 percent in some caves. The fungus appears to weaken and kill the bats during their most vulnerable time—the long, cold winter hibernation period. Even though Tuttle has officially retired as president and executive director of BCI, he is still working with his organization to figure out what's needed to respond to this present extinction threat.

"The loss of bats could seriously threaten whole ecosystems," says Tuttle. "But we've come a long way since I started tagging gray bats back in the 1950s. A lot more people now understand the importance of bats. And as a result, we're making more progress in protecting them, though challenges like white-nose syndrome remain very serious. We need a lot more bat crusaders."

ROSAMIRA GUILLEN
COTTON-TOP TAMARIN

"These tiny creatures are taken from the wild to be sold as pets. I can understand why people would want to have one, but we must turn this self-centered caring into conservation support for the wild populations."

Cotton-Top Tamarin

→ **Scientific Name:** *Saguinus oedipus*

→ **Range:** Found only in tropical forests of northern Colombia, now restricted to patches surrounded by farmland and pastures. An estimated 1.5 percent of dry forest habitat remains.

→ **Population Trend:** Declining. Estimates reveal a greater than 80 percent population decline in the past 20 years. Fewer than 6,000 individuals are thought to remain.

→ **IUCN Status:** Critically Endangered

Rosamira Guillen

→ **Education:** Advanced degree in environmental management from the Universidad Politécnica de Madrid, Columbia

→ **Nationality:** Colombian

→ **Organizational Affiliation:** Fundación Proyecto Tití

→ **Years Working with Cotton-top Tamarins:** 10

→ **Honors:** "The Young Outstanding People" Award—Junior Chamber International (2008); Sociedad Colombiana de Arquitectos Atlántico, Recognition to Excellence in Professional Development (2005); "Outstanding Women" Award—Asociación Día Internacional de la Mujer (2005)

→ **Notable Accomplishments:** Executive director of Fundación Proyecto Tití; former president of Colombian Association of Zoos and Aquariums; former executive director of the Barranquilla Botanical and Zoological Foundation; Wildlife Conservation Network partner

ROSAMIRA Guillen began her professional career as an architect, designing homes for people, but found her passion through preserving the homes of the cotton-top tamarin. "I couldn't believe I had never even heard of these cute, endangered little monkeys in my life until I began to design a remodel of a local zoo," she says. "After all, I was born and raised in Colombia, the only country in the world where cotton-top tamarins are found. It was love at first sight!"

Colombia covers less than 1 percent of the planet's land surface, but holds approximately 10 percent of its plant and animal species. The forests are, however, some of the most heavily damaged in the world, and very little of this monkey's historical range remains. "Being a citizen of a country that is so rich in biodiversity, such as Colombia, makes me really proud," says Guillen, "but it also makes me responsible for doing something to protect its wildlife and wild places." Guillen has definitely risen to the challenge. She directs the local and international efforts of Proyecto Tití, an organization founded in 1985 by Disney Animal Kingdom's Anne Savage, to protect the cotton-top tamarin.

What You Should Know about Tamarins

→ Tamarins are squirrel-sized monkeys only found in South and Central America.

→ Although tamarins look very similar to the marmoset—another small monkey of the Western Hemisphere—their teeth set them apart.

→ Cotton-top tamarins have an unusually sophisticated repertoire of 38 distinct vocalizations used to express needs and emotions.

→ Males and siblings do the majority of caring for offspring, since mom needs help after giving birth to twins, together weighing almost 15 percent of her weight.

→ Cotton-top tamarins are one of the most endangered primates in the world.

Why It Is Important to Save Cotton-Top Tamarins

Tamarins are important seed dispersers in their forest habitat. These tiny primates eat fruits and seeds in a quantity and size that even many larger animals don't consume.

Guillen's main goal is to prevent further loss of the cotton-top's forest home. She does this by educating the communities surrounding the tiny primate's habitat and through community-based conservation projects. "It's not enough to just teach about the importance of forests and animals to people who have so little," she says. "So we provide them with training, tools, and ideas to reduce their impact on the forests. They have a better life—and so do the tamarins."

Since forests provide fuel, food, and materials for local residents to survive, Guillen and Savage needed to provide alternative sources for obtaining these necessary items. One project, which offers a regular income for women living around the forest, involves making eco-*mochilas*. Guillen explains: "*Mochilas* are traditional bags used widely in Colombia. We came up with the idea of making these totes from plastic bags left as trash in and around the forest areas. The women collect bags, clean up the environment, and through their artwork and skill, create beautiful and useful carry-alls to sell. It's been incredibly successful."

The women in these working collectives are very attuned to the fact that the continued presence of cotton-top tamarins is key to the support they've received from Proyecto Tití to establish their eco-mochila business. "Recently a group of women from the collective spotted strangers entering their forest," explains Guillen. "The women knew that the strangers were most likely there to steal cotton-top tamarins and sell them in the city, so they ran back to the village and got a large group to come back and chase the poachers out of their forest."

Cotton-top tamarins are one of the world's smallest primates, averaging less than a pound. Regardless of their small size, they are important seed dispersers in the forest because they consume not only large quantities and varieties of fruits

and seeds but also large-*sized* ones that even much larger animals don't eat. Seeds that have traveled through the cotton-top's intestines have a very high germination success rate. "It's not a one-way street. These little guys really help the forest." Cotton-tops also regularly consume insects and, when available, sap from trees as a source of minerals and nutrients.

Unfortunately, 99 percent of the cotton-top tamarins' original forest habitat has been destroyed. With so little territory still intact, they must at times travel across cleared areas to reach other forest fragments, leaving them vulnerable. As small as they are, tamarins must be extremely vigilant. Living in social groups and making sure there is always someone on watch helps, but not for all their threats. "Besides having their own natural

predators, such as hawks and snakes, and the constant pressure of habitat loss and degradation, these tiny creatures are also taken from the wild to be sold as pets. I can understand why people would want to have one, but we must turn this self-centered caring into conservation support for the wild populations," says Guillen.

These primates were also exported to the United States by the tens of thousands in the early 1970s for use in biomedical research. Now it's estimated that there may be fewer than six thousand left in the wild. Guillen knows each individual is important in a population this low. "We monitor population trends, behavior, and movements," she says, "but it's not easy with animals this small and quick." In order to facilitate data gathering, Proyecto Tití has come up with several unique techniques. "We actually mark some animals with brightly colored human hair dye once a year," says Guillen. "That way we can spot them through the dense vegetation." The team also fits each dominant male with tiny radio transmitters worn in a backpack-type harness. These harnesses fit snugly enough to not get caught in branches and also allow for the males to still carry infants, which is an important role males play in rearing offspring.

"Not knowing anything about Colombia's cotton-topped tamarins until I was an adult has really made me aware of the challenges we are facing. I now need to make up time and do everything possible to ensure that the future of 'South America's cutest monkey' is secure."

FELICITY ARENGO
SOUTH AMERICAN FLAMINGOS

"Flamingos can stand all day long in water that would burn the flesh off a human, they eat upside down using a nifty filtering system in their mouths, and the species of flamingos I study can withstand freezing temperatures at high altitudes."

FAST FACTS

Flamingos

→ **Species:** Six flamingo species belong to three closely related genera: The genus *Phoenicopterus* includes the *P. roseus* (greater flamingo) and the *P. chilensis* (Chilean flamingo). The genus *Phoeniconaias* includes *P. ruber* (American flamingo) and *P. minor* (lesser flamingo). The genus *Phoenicoparrus* includes the *P. andinus* (Andean flamingo) and *P. jamesi* (James's or Puna flamingo).

→ **Range:** Four species are found in the Americas: the Andean and Puna in the Andes Mountains; the Chilean in more temperate regions of South America; and the American, or Caribbean, flamingo, which ranges throughout the Caribbean, Galápagos Islands, Colombia, and Venezuela. Two species are found in Africa, Europe, and India.

→ **Population Trend:** Declining for the lesser flamingo of Africa and the three Southern Cone species, the Andean, Chilean, and Puna flamingo. The greater flamingo and Caribbean species are both stable.

→ **IUCN Status:** The Andean is the most seriously threatened, with a Vulnerable listing. The lesser, Chilean, and Puna species are Near Threatened. The final two species are listed as Least Concern.

Felicity Arengo

→ **Education:** PhD from the State University of New York College of Environmental Science and Forestry

→ **Nationality:** Argentinean and American

→ **Organizational Affiliation:** American Museum of Natural History

→ **Years Working with Flamingo Conservation:** 18

→ **Publications:** Contributed the chapter *Flamingos* to the book *Wildlife Spectacles*

→ **Notable Accomplishments:** Associate director of the Center for Biodiversity and Conservation at the American Museum of Natural History; Americas coordinator for the IUCN Flamingo Specialist Group; founding member, Grupo Conservación de Flamencos Altoandinos (GCFA); advisor, Ciconiiformes Taxon Advisory Group; editor for Flamingo Bulletin of the IUCN-SSC/Wetlands International Flamingo Specialist Group

FELICITY Arengo has always been drawn to mystery and adventure, even as a child. She grew up asking questions and seeking answers—in particular about the world outdoors. Fortunately these interests have lent themselves well to a career studying one of the most popular yet unusual, inaccessible, and mysterious birds in nature—the flamingo.

Flamingos are thought of by many as one of the most beautiful birds in nature—not just because of their stunning colors, which vary from delicate pink to bright orange, but because of their size and design. Most people associate the flamingo with tropical climates and Caribbean flair, but flamingos are also hardy birds that live in some of the harshest conditions on Earth. They have evolved over millions of years to perfect their adaptations to unforgiving environments. Arengo explains, "Flamingos can stand all day long in water that would burn the flesh right off a human, they eat upside down using a nifty filtering system in their mouths, and the species of flamingos I study can withstand freezing temperatures at high altitudes."

The family of birds called flamingos, which are separated into six species, is typically found only in areas containing shallow, alkaline, or saline lakes. These lakes are rich in the foods they prefer—small crustaceans, algae, and other tiny aquatic organisms that they filter out of the water using *lamellae*—fine, hairlike protrusions that line their unusual-looking bills. Lesser flamingos, the most numerous of the flamingo species, are found in the Rift Valley of Kenya and Tanzania; the greater flamingo ranges from parts of Africa to southern Europe and India; and the Caribbean or American flamingo is found in the islands of the Bahamas, Galapagos, and Cuba, as well as in Mexico and Venezuela. The other three species, which Arengo studies alongside her South American colleagues, can be found at least part of the year high in the Andes Mountains, on the *Altiplano*, which spans four countries: Chile, Argentina, Bolivia, and Peru.

In order to obtain accurate surveys and establish the habitat needs of the South American flamingo, Arengo is required to prepare for the most harsh and inhospitable conditions. "We pack for twenty degrees below and over two

Why It Is Important To Save Flamingos

Flamingos are one of the few animals that can survive in the extremely salty wetlands in which they thrive. Flamingos stir up and transfer nutrients when they stomp to loosen and raise food, eat, and defecate. The birds and their eggs are a source of protein for predators living in the same areas.

miles up in altitude," she says. "We take cold-weather gear and oxygen tanks with us, and the flamingos are already up there, occasionally hanging close to the hot springs but walking over ice at times to eat." The Andean, Chilean, and Puna (or alternately called James's) flamingos all utilize the high-altitude lakes of the Andes for at least part of their habitat needs. Here, until relatively recently, they have had few predators and little disturbance, except for what they have gotten from determined researchers. But however remote, these lakes are surprisingly still under threat from mining, road construction, and urbanization. And something Arengo has discovered makes the situation even worse: the flamingos use lower-altitude environments as well—and those are under heavy pressure from development. "The crucial element the birds need are the wetlands—it's where they find their food, stay safe from predation, build nests, and raise their young," she explains. Unfortunately, mining, cattle grazing, unregulated hunting, egg collection, gas and power lines, and agriculture are destroying these critical habitats. Thankfully, Arengo and her colleagues are working to halt this destruction.

Arengo is a member of the Grupo de Conservación de Flamencos Altoandinos (GCFA), a regional conservation initiative, to design and establish a network of high-value wetlands for the conservation of flamingos. Arengo and the GCFA collaborate with locals to train park guards, raise awareness in the resident population, and work with decision makers to increase wetlands protection. "Flamingos are great, charismatic, attention-getting icons for wetlands. And when we obtain protection for them, we get it for all the life that this unique environment sustains—including the invertebrates, fish, smaller birds, and mammals that also depend on these wetlands for their survival," says Arengo.

What You Should Know about Flamingos

→ Flamingos live in large, noisy groups and nest in colonies, at some locations numbering in the millions.

→ Flamingos can safely drink the salty and near-boiling water that can be found in the hot springs and geysers where they live.

→ Flamingo parents—both the male and the female—produce a red liquid called "crop milk," a substance high in fat and protein for their hungry chick.

→ The orange or pink coloration of adult birds comes from their diet of crustaceans and algae, both of which contain beta carotene

→ Flamingos may not breed every year and are easily disturbed, adding to other threats of habitat loss and degradation, collection of eggs, and hunting.

Arengo also heads up Americas Region for the Flamingo Specialist Group. In this capacity she coordinates action plans, research, and conservation activities for these birds among the dozens of scientists and others that are working to learn more about how to protect flamingos and their habitats.

Arengo and a multinational team of researchers have spent some of the coldest weeks of the year counting flamingos in the Altiplano. "It's not until we know how many birds there are in these harshest of environments, if populations are increasing or decreasing, and if they leave during certain times of the year, that we can determine how important the lower-altitude habitats are," Arengo explains. "You only learn these things by putting in the time studying the animal where it lives. Once we know the answers to these and lots of other crucial questions, we'll begin to know how best to protect the flamingos of South America."

Flamingos are unpredictable in their movements and range over vast areas, so Arengo has satellite-tracked birds to discover where they go. This technology has allowed her to find new sites important to their survival. Her research has shown that one of the largest lakes in the region, Laguna Melincué, also appears to be one of the most important, with flamingos appearing every year. Smaller wetlands, however, seem to be critical "satellite" sites, visited depending on the current environmental conditions. "We have initially proposed nineteen different wetland sites for protection necessary to conserve South America's flamingos," says Arengo. "Individual flamingos do not use just one site—they are itinerant—utilizing different wetlands as resources are available. They need a suite of sites on an annual basis, and over their life cycle." Thanks to the awareness and data the GCFA have provided, Laguna Melincué is now recognized as a wetland of international importance under the Ramsar Convention, as is one area of the higher Altiplano lakes, Lagunas Altoandinas y Puneñas de Catamarca. Unfortunately, many of the other identified priority habitats are not protected and will take additional work to conserve.

Of all the flamingo species, the Andean flamingo is considered the most threatened, numbering at just an estimated thirty-five thousand birds. The closely related Puna and Chilean flamingos are both listed as Near Threatened. "We are just now getting a handle on population sizes as a result of the GCFA censuses, and can begin to monitor population trends, while implementing additional protections to habitats, the birds, and their eggs during nesting season." Arengo is optimistic that her favorite birds will have a more secure future, knowing that she and her colleagues are together committed to finding the answers needed to conserve flamingos and their habitats. As a child, Arengo asked a lot of questions. Now she's able to provide the answers to make sure no child will ever have to ask, "What happened to the beautiful pink birds that used to live here?"

SIEW TE WONG
SUN BEAR

"I often call sun bears the 'forgotten species': little known and rarely seen."

FAST FACTS

Sun Bear

→ **Scientific Name:** *Ursus malayanus*

→ **Range:** Although sun bears have been extirpated from many parts of their natural range, they can still be found in eleven Southeast Asian countries, including the islands of Borneo and Sumatra.

→ **Population Trend:** While exact population numbers are difficult to determine given the sun bear's elusive habits, the population is considered to be decreasing in the face of rapid habitat loss and an active black-market trade in bear parts.

→ **IUCN Status:** Vulnerable

Siew Te Wong

→ **Education:** PhD from the University of Montana

→ **Nationality:** Malaysian

→ **Organizational Affiliation:** Bornean Sun Bear Conservation Center

→ **Years Working with Sun Bears:** 14

→ **Honors:** Fellow of the Flying Elephants Foundation (2007)

→ **Notable Accomplishments:** Founder of the Borneo Sun Bear Conservation Center in Sabah, Malaysian Borneo; former cochair of the Sun Bear Experts Team under the IUCN's Species Survival Commission Bear Specialist Group

SIEW Te Wong has known since the first grade that he wanted to devote his life to working with animals, although it wasn't until college that he found his destiny: studying and protecting one of the least-researched large mammals in the world: the sun bear.

Growing up in the state of Penang in northern Peninsular Malaysia, Wong went from raising pets at home to studying animal husbandry and veterinary medicine at a university in Taiwan. Eventually, he took a position as a research assistant studying Taiwanese wildlife, which ultimately led him to his work with the mysterious sun bear on the island of Borneo.

"When I first started investigating the lives of sun bears in Borneo in 1998, no one had ever tried to study the species there before. I soon learned why—the bears are secretive by nature, and the jungle itself presents many obstacles to successful field research," says Wong. "It's wet, hot, and humid, with dense foliage that makes it hard to see anything. And the jungle is filled with blood-sucking bugs and leeches, and even plants that will attack you with thorns and poisons. To work there, you must know the rules of the forest—do not touch anything, sit on anything, or lean on anything. Everything there has evolved to fight back."

That same year Wong began his own study in Borneo for his master's in science, then returned in 2005 to the same study area for his PhD work on

What You Should Know about Sun Bears

→ Sun bears are the smallest, most arboreal, and least known of the world's eight bear species.

→ The name *sun bear* comes from the light-colored marking on their chests, which has been said to resemble a rising or setting sun.

→ The unique physical attributes of sun bears—long tongues and claws, big feet, and a slight build—all increase their success in climbing and foraging in the trees.

→ Sun bears have a history of being exploited in Southeast Asia and India for entertainment, the pet trade, and for use in traditional Asian medicine.

Why It Is Important to Save Sun Bears

Because of their omnivorous diet, sun bears play an important role in some regions as seed dispersers—dropping undigested seeds throughout the forest along with natural fertilizer in their feces.

the sun bear and bearded pig. In both cases he used equipment and techniques such as camera traps, barrel traps, and collection of bear scat to document the range and density of sun bears in Borneo. "It turns out the pygmy elephants of Borneo react aggressively to anything unnatural in their environment," he says. "Several times we returned to camp and found things like the camera traps, the barrel traps, even my truck—smashed by jungle elephants that visited while we were away. They call Borneo elephants 'pygmy' elephants, but they are still strong enough and big enough to damage anything I can bring into the jungle."

In addition to the inconveniences of jungle research, there are also dangers. The wet, rainy conditions are not only hard on the equipment and researchers, but can wash out roads and bridges and cause mudslides and landslides. Tragically, in 2007 one of Wong's research assistants drowned while conducting field work. But despite this devastating setback, Wong has continued to study sun bears for almost two decades.

"My entire time studying them," he says, "I have only actually been able to temporarily capture and restrain ten individual bears for collecting biological samples, which should give you an idea how hard they are to find." Wong adds, "I often call sun bears the 'forgotten species': little known and rarely seen."

Sun bears—whose name comes from the light-colored crescent-shaped patch on their chests that can sometimes resemble a setting or rising sun—are the smallest in the bear family. Males are bigger than females and only average about one hundred pounds. Many of the sun bear's physical features are adaptations to its arboreal existence in a tropical climate—long, four-inch claws; big feet and small body size; small ears; and short but dense fur. Sun bears also have an incredibly long, slender tongue for obtaining honey from beehives; however, these bears are omnivores, so they eat whatever they can find, from insects, lizards, birds, and eggs to plant shoots, berries, roots, and nuts.

Sun bears are in decline throughout their range from many of the same threats that affect other rainforest wildlife, such as habitat loss from logging, agriculture, and a growing human population. They are also sold unlawfully in the pet trade and hunted illegally for meat and their gall bladders, which are used in traditional Chinese medicines.

As Wong became known in Southeast Asia for his sun bear work, people began to come to him with stories of captive sun bears being kept in deplorable conditions. The more he looked into these reports, the more he found the captive circumstances to be just as appalling as he had feared. After seeing this over and over again, he determined to do something about it, so he began plans for the Borneo Sun Bear Conservation Center. The Center provides facilities for rescuing and housing captive bears, increasing public awareness locally and internationally about this mammal, and rehabilitating bears for release back into the wild whenever possible.

"It is heartbreaking to see so many captive sun bears treated so poorly, and sometimes it seems like we're losing the battle to save wild populations as well," says Wong. "But I feel I was chosen for this work, so I will keep with it as long as it takes to help save this species—the forgotten bear—and the other magnificent creatures of the Borneo rainforest."

DEBORAH TABART
KOALA

"If you cannot save the koala, who does not destroy crops, does not destroy livestock, does not attack—just sits beautifully in a gum tree—then it will be impossible to save any of our nature."

Koala

→ **Scientific Name:** *Phascolarctos cinereus*

→ **Range:** Found in forested habitat of easternmost and southeast Australia

→ **Population Trend:** It is thought that there are now between 43,000 and 80,000 individual koalas, down from numbers believed to be in the millions prior to European settlement.

→ **IUCN Status:** Least Concern; however, U.S. government has listed it as Threatened on the U.S. list of foreign species under the Endangered Species Act, and it is listed as Vulnerable in New South Wales and Southeast Queensland.

Deborah Tabart

→ **Nationality:** Australian

→ **Organizational Affiliation:** Australian Koala Foundation

→ **Years Working with Koalas:** 23

→ **Honors:** International Association of Business Communicators' Excellence in Communication Leadership Award (2011); awarded the Order of Australia Medal (2008); Equity Trustees Not-for-Profit CEO of the Year Long Term Achiever award (2008); Computerworld Smithsonian Medal for excellence in mapping technology (1998)

→ **Notable Accomplishments:** CEO of Australian Koala Foundation; primary architect of the Koala Habitat Atlas; in partnership with the Ray Group, created "Koala Beach," a koala-friendly community in New South Wales; founder of Enviromap the World company

NATIONAL Public Radio (NPR) correspondent Alex Chadwick once described koala conservationist Deb Tabart as the love child of General Patton and Mother Teresa. Tabart has approached the conservation of Australia's koalas with such fearlessness and passion that she has certainly earned this formidable reputation. Tabart—known internationally as the "Koala Woman" by those who know koalas—is recognized in her country for her trademark fire-red lipstick and business suits, an unusual persona for an environmentalist and crusader. A former beauty queen, Tabart accepted the position of executive director of the Australian Koala Foundation in 1988 and proceeded to build the organization into one of the most powerful advocacy and science-based groups Down Under.

In particular, Tabart has used the science of mapping to propel the cause of koala conservation forward. With the company she founded, called Enviromap the World, she has developed cutting-edge vegetation mapping techniques to prove to the Australian government that koalas are, in fact, imperiled—and what must be done and where, to ensure the future existence of this much-beloved species in Australia. Her use of volunteer teams to ground-truth satellite vegetation imagery has

What You Should Know about Koalas

→ The commonly used name "koala bear" is a misnomer, as koalas are actually marsupials, closer related to the wombat than to bears.

→ The collective name for a group of koalas is a *colony*. Koalas have a strong social structure.

→ Koalas sleep 18 to 22 hours a day.

→ Koalas—and the squirrel-like marsupials called sugar gliders—are the only mammals that can digest the toxins found in eucalyptus leaves, which are their principal food source.

enabled her to definitively show decision makers and skeptics every last tree in Australia that can support koalas, mapping vegetation on more than 4 million hectares (fifteen hundred square miles) of land. These efforts won Tabart a Computerworld Smithsonian Medal for excellence in mapping technology in 1998.

Koalas have coevolved alongside their principal dietary staple, the eucalyptus tree, for millions of years. Since white settlement, roughly 80 percent of koala habitat has been destroyed. Most of what remains is unprotected on privately owned land. Koalas are threatened principally by habitat loss due to urbanization and logging, but motor vehicle strikes, dog attacks, fire, insecticides, and other man-made threats also challenge their continued existence. Under Tabart's leadership the Australian Koala Foundation has launched programs to address all these issues, using education, outreach, and strident advocacy when necessary to be heard in a country where koalas are still considered common by many, despite a steady decline in numbers over the past few decades.

"It's not just about the koalas—although they are incredibly important to Australia's identity in their own right," says Tabart. "If you cannot save the koala, who does not destroy crops, does not destroy livestock, does not attack—just sits beautifully in a gum tree—then it will be impossible to save any of our nature. If there is not enough will to save an animal as beloved and harmless as the koala, how can we even begin to address conservation needs for animals like lions and elephants that come into conflict with humans regularly?"

Although Tabart has frequently gone toe to toe with developers to protect koalas and their habitat, she masterminded the first koala-friendly development complex in New South Wales, known as "Koala Beach"—a community where koalas live alongside residents who have changed their lifestyles to include koala needs and safety. To maintain harmony between the residents and wild

Why It Is Important to Save the Koala

The koala is the symbol of Australia. It is estimated to be contributing between $1.1 and $2.5 billion dollars annually to Australia's economy through koala-linked tourism, koala-viewing industry revenue, and purchases of "koalabilia," which translates into 9,000 jobs for Australians.

koalas, Tabart's group did a thorough study of the koala population prior to development, and then working closely with the development company, created guidelines calling for speed bumps, a ban on cats and dogs, koala-accessible fencing, and most important, a requirement that no koala home range or food tree be removed for development purposes. As a result, out of a total 365 hectares, more than 272 hectares on Koala Beach were left intact and dedicated to conservation (a little over a square mile).

Most recently, Tabart has written and is working to pass a piece of national legislation to provide real protections for koalas currently lacking in federal and state legislation in Australia. The bill provides incentives for private landowners to preserve koala habitat, and also puts responsibility on the government to ensure that viable koala habitats remain on public lands. Ultimately, strong koala protections will benefit Australian citizens as well as koalas, as these tree-dwelling mammals are estimated to bring more than $1.1 billion in tourist revenue to Australia's economy every year.

In 2008 Tabart was awarded the Order of Australia Medal, one of the highest honors possible in Australia, equivalent to a knighting in England. The medal was awarded in recognition of Tabart's successful use of science and savvy statesmanship to keep koalas safe, and in the media and political forefront both in her country, and internationally, as a means to protect and preserve them.

GEORGE ARCHIBALD
CRANES

"The first time I saw cranes migrating, I was mesmerized... After all these years, it's still exciting when I see cranes flying overhead."

Cranes

→ **Scientific Name:** There are 15 species of cranes, which make up the family of birds called Gruidae.

→ **Range:** Wetland and grassland environments around the world except for Antarctica and South America

→ **Population Trend:** Cranes are among the most endangered family of birds worldwide. Some species, thanks to conservation efforts, are increasing slowly.

→ **IUCN Status:** Six species of crane are listed as Vulnerable, two as Endangered, and one—the Siberian—as Critically Endangered.

George Archibald

→ **Education:** PhD from Cornell University

→ **Nationality:** Canadian

→ **Organizational Affiliation:** International Crane Foundation

→ **Years Working on Cranes:** 45+

→ **Honors:** Nature Canada's Douglas H. Pimlott Award (2007); Inaugural Indianapolis Prize winner (2006); Wisconsin Conservation Hall of Fame (2006); the Zoological Society of San Diego's Wildlife Conservation Medal (2005); added to the United Nations Global 500 Roll of Honour (1987); recipient of MacArthur Foundation's Fellows Award (1984)

→ **Books Published:** Coauthored *The Cranes: Status Survey and Conservation Action Plan for the International Union for the Conservation of Nature*

→ **Notable Accomplishments:** Cofounder of the International Crane Foundation; helped pioneer crane conservation rearing with costumed handlers, and the use of ultralight aircraft to facilitate migration; spearheaded efforts resulting in 5 million hectares (more than nineteen thousand square miles) of important crane wetland habitat being conserved in Asia

GEORGE Archibald is a wildlife scientist who enjoys being around people just as much as he does birds. So, being a social animal himself, it is not surprising that he was drawn to work with cranes—a species known for their complex mating rituals and social behaviors. "The Canadian naturalist Al Oeming revealed the world of cranes to me at a game farm in northern Alberta in 1966. Al told me, 'There are apes and man, and birds and cranes,'—I was hooked," says Archibald.

By the time he was introduced to cranes, almost half of the world's fifteen crane species were endangered. Extinction seemed inevitable for some—most markedly the North American whooping crane, which was reduced to just fifteen birds in a migratory flock in 1940.

The graceful sight and synchronized duets of cranes led Archibald to an advanced degree in the unison vocalizations of these birds. From there, he and fellow Cornell University graduate Ron Sauey created the International Crane Foundation (ICF) in 1973, dedicated to the preservation and research of crane species worldwide. "Of all the things I have done in my life, including helping cranes in the wild around the world and meeting many fascinating people, founding ICF has been by far my greatest contribution to the future survival of cranes," states Archibald. Partly through this organization, people all over the world are coordinating information and efforts. "If conservation programs continue and grow, all crane species should thrive."

Those crane species with the greatest need for large expanses of wetland habitat, such as the whooping, red-crowned, and Siberian, are under the most pressure due to loss of wetlands caused by humans. Other species have proved more adaptable and are thriving, such as sandhills, the most numerous crane species, and Demoiselles, which can inhabit drier grasslands.

Archibald, through knowledge, persistence, and creativity, helped pioneer several breakthrough techniques in the rearing of cranes in human care prior to release into the wild. ICF accommodated researcher Dr. Robert Horwich's work to develop a technique for successfully releasing captive reared cranes by dressing caretakers in crane costumes to avoid the birds imprinting on humans instead of their own species. And as a member of the Whooping Crane Recovery Team, George introduced to his colleagues the amazing work of fellow Canadians Bill Lishman and Joe Duff, who used ultralight airplanes to teach young cranes new migration routes.

Archibald even spent three years as the surrogate "mate" of a lone, human-imprinted whooping crane. By dressing and acting like a crane, he coaxed "Tex," a female crane, to come into breeding

What You Should Know about Cranes

→ The whooping crane was one of the first bird species to be added to the United States Endangered Species Act of 1973.

→ Two species are found in North America—the sandhill, which is the most numerous crane species, and the whooping crane, one of the most endangered.

→ All crane species have elaborate "dance" movements, which are thought to strengthen pair bonds, relieve stress, and reduce aggression among the flock.

→ Sarus cranes are the world's tallest flying birds.

→ Cranes stand on one leg while roosting, with the other leg tucked into their bodies, to keep warm.

condition, and then used artificial insemination to produce a fertile egg, which hatched, grew, and eventually fathered seven critical offspring of its own. The story was so unique and compelling that Archibald was asked to present it on a segment of *The Tonight Show* and drew much-needed attention and funding to crane conservation.

Archibald has had his share of heartbreak over his favorite birds as well. Tex was killed by a pack of raccoons soon after producing her one chick. And in 1978, a virus infected the flock, reducing numbers available for future breeding by more than half. "Tragedy pushed us to find new allies and build ICF into an even stronger and more effective organization. From that tragedy we had a rebirth and have just continued to grow," relates Archibald.

The northernmost species of cranes, which includes whooping crane, are extraordinarily migratory, some species flying distances greater than four hundred miles in a single day and ten thousand miles round-trip. Chicks must acquire the size, strength, and endurance to make this journey with their parents in their first year—an amazing feat for any animal.

Archibald remembers his first experience seeing cranes in the wild: "The first time I saw cranes migrating, I was mesmerized. I heard them before I saw them, in their characteristic kettling formations flying over northern Alberta. It was spectacular. After all these years, it's still exciting when I see cranes flying overhead."

Cranes can climb as high as thirty thousand feet to cross over the highest mountains on Earth, but need to build up fat reserves prior to these strenuous journeys. They also need places to rest and refuel along the way. Without crucial habitat available for rest stops along the way, spread out across the many different countries over which the cranes will fly, the birds cannot succeed. Approximately 60 percent of wetlands worldwide have been lost due to drainage for agriculture and development, pollution, peat extraction, and other human causes. Cranes are dependent on wetlands to feed, rest, and nest. But wetlands are important in their natural state for humans as well—as a source and purifier of drinking water, a hatchery for countless fish and crustacean species, and for flood control.

Archibald, the people person who loves and acts on behalf of birds, has a positive view of it all. "By helping cranes survive, we are helping to save wetland ecosystems and to encourage international cooperation, all of which helps ourselves as well."

Why It Is Important to Save Cranes

The omnivorous crane helps control insect and small vertebrate numbers (such as rodents, frogs, and small snakes) and vegetation density in the wetlands and grasslands where it lives. Cranes and their eggs are also prey for predators such as foxes, wild cats, crocodiles, large snakes, and ravens.

MARC ANCRENAZ
BORNEAN ORANGUTAN

"Anybody, if given a chance, can become a scientist or conservation hero if they just have passion, drive, and a little guidance. It's what the orangutan is counting on."

FAST FACTS

Orangutans

→ **Scientific Name:** *Pongo pygmaeus*; *Pongo abelii*

→ **Range:** Originally found throughout Indonesia and Malaysia, Java, Vietnam, and China, but now restricted to Borneo and Sumatra

→ **Population Trend:** Declining, with an estimated 6,500 individuals in Sumatra, and another 50,000 to 60,000 individuals in Borneo

→ **IUCN Status:** The Bornean species is listed as Endangered, while the Sumatran is Critically Endangered.

Marc Ancrenaz

→ **Education:** Doctor of Veterinary Medicine, École Vétérinaire de Maisons-Alfort, France

→ **Nationality:** French

→ **Organizational Affiliation:** HUTAN-Kinabatangan Orangutan Conservation Project

→ **Years Working with Bornean Orangutans:** 18

→ **Notable Accomplishments:** Cofounder of the HUTAN-Kinabatangan Orangutan Conservation Project; member of the steering committee for Zoos and Aquariums: Committing to Conservation conference; developed Red Ape Encounters with locals, who benefit from tourism and help preserve wildlife habitat

MARC Ancrenaz doesn't know from where his love for animals generated. Born in Paris, France, with no special exposure to wild animals, he just knew he wanted to be—and work—around wildlife. He first became a veterinarian and worked with all sorts of fascinating animals in Africa and the Middle East—gorillas, aye-ayes, mandrills, ostriches, Arabian oryx, and others. He also developed a profound respect for the local people who lived with many of these species right in their own backyards. Says Ancrenaz, "I realized long ago that members of local communities can become the best defenders of wildlife if proper training and opportunities are given to them. They are the true heroes, sometimes risking their lives to protect these species we love so much in the Western world without really knowing the costs of sharing their natural habitat."

Ancrenaz and his wife, Isabelle Lackman-Ancrenaz, visited Borneo for the first time in 1994 when the accepted knowledge about orangutans was that they needed pristine, intact forests in which to survive in the wild. What the couple saw were orangutan nests in degraded areas where humans had significantly changed the natural forest. That piqued their interest, and together with a French grassroots nonprofit organization called HUTAN and the Sabah Wildlife Department, the

What You Should Know about Orangutans

→ Orangutans are the largest arboreal (tree-dwelling) animal on Earth.

→ Adult male orangutans have large cheek pads called *flanges*, thought to be useful in amplifying the long, loud call of the male for territoriality and finding mates.

→ Orangutans can build up to two nests every day of folded-over leaves and branches, one for naptime and one for sleeping overnight. Most youngsters up to eight years old will sleep in their mother's nest.

→ Orangutans are known to make umbrellas out of huge forest plant leaves when it rains, and chew leaves into absorbable sponges to soak up water in hard-to-get places.

Why It Is Important to Save Orangutans

Orangutans disperse a wide variety of plant seeds to aid in the regeneration of their forest habitat. They also control damaging caterpillar incursions. And because orangutans require large areas of suitable habitat, their protection helps countless other species as well. Orangutans are also one of humans' closest living relatives.

HUTAN-Kinabatangan Orangutan Conservation Project (KOCP) soon followed. Today, the Ancrenazes have demonstrated that orangutans can, in fact, survive in degraded, fragmented forest—if food is available and they are not hunted, which is still a major threat, especially on private or unprotected lands. While Marc and Isabelle showed that orangutans are far more adaptable than first thought, 60 percent do still live outside of protected areas, and their conservation is complex at best. "We need to develop a landscape approach that brings together not only wildlife managers and scientists, but politicians, the private sector, and the villagers. We need to think outside the box to come up with strategies where local communities can benefit from their natural resources in a more sustainable way," states Ancrenaz.

Orangutans certainly are an engaging species, which can benefit from tourism, as long as local villages can profit as well. Just in the past couple of decades, lodges have sprung up, only some of which ultimately help orangutans. Red Ape Encounters is one of the few community-owned tour companies, whose guides and researchers were trained by KOCP, offering authentic bed-and-breakfast stays in the homes of the locals. Marc and Isabelle encourage potential visitors to experience a real Borneo community that gives back benefits directly to local villagers who in turn become the guardians and defenders of orangutans. Fees and employment received by Red Ape Encounters support education, and protection of wildlife and habitat.

KOCP is also engaged in several diverse outreach initiatives. One of these projects is targeted at the fishing community, which has adopted a more eco-friendly fish trap made of recycled materials rather than forest tree bark, which regularly needed to be replaced.

Legend has it that orangutans are simply people who went to live in the trees to avoid work or slavery, which explains the meaning of their name, *orangutans*—literally, "people of the forest" in

the Malay language. They are the only great ape in Asia and are currently found on one of two island habitats in the wild—Borneo and Sumatra. Orangutans claim many unique characteristics—they are the only largely arboreal ape species, living virtually their whole lives fifty or more feet in the treetops. And no other great ape comes close to the striking red coloration of this unique animal with the reputation as the "thinker" of the world of higher primates.

Orangutans eat a wide variety of foods from different plants, including three hundred types of fruits, as well as insects. Finding enough food often means traveling great distances each day. Just maneuvering efficiently and safely through dense forest takes years to master. In order to learn all an orangutan needs to survive, a youngster will stay with its mother for eight years or longer. Adult females will hold off having more offspring until the

first one is well on its way to becoming independent; thus, orangutans have the longest inter-birth interval of any mammal on Earth. Due to this extended nurturing period, females may only give birth to four or five babies in their lifetimes.

Ancrenaz believes in the value of nature that goes beyond most people's natural affiliation. "I find the orangutan an incredible animal so worthy of our protection. And I firmly believe conservationists need to commit ten, twenty, or more years to effectively work with the local communities to develop a strategy that will work to save species and habitat in the long run, not just while we may be present."

Believing in the capabilities of the local residents is not just a theoretical viewpoint. The KOCP research team is made up of fifty research assistants, all of whom are from the communities surrounding the Kinabatangan floodplain—a vital habitat area for the orangutan. Most of these researchers began with little formal schooling, some having to leave school as early as the sixth grade, but now they uncover and record new data, design their own projects, and share results with the scientific world. The fact that the locals are playing such a huge role in conserving resources, planning conservation strategy, and protecting "their" orangutans bodes well for a species that needs human intervention in a positive direction if they are to continue to survive. Ancrenaz reflects, "It is an amazing process to realize that anybody, if given a chance, can become a scientist or conservation hero if they just have passion, drive, and a little guidance. It's what the orangutan is counting on."

FIRE

WORKING ON THE MOST CRITICAL WILDLIFE ISSUES

CHAPTER INTRODUCTION

BY JAY INSLEE, ENVIRONMENTAL ADVOCATE, CONGRESSIONAL REPRESENTATIVE, AND COAUTHOR OF *APOLLO'S FIRE: IGNITING AMERICA'S CLEAN ENERGY ECONOMY*

The Tiger's Eye and the Paintbrush Flower

The infinite absence caused by extinction represents such a profound loss it is difficult for us to fully understand. There are, however, moments when you catch a glimpse of it, with the painful insight of its irreversibility and permanence impossible to ignore.

Fifteen years ago I looked directly into the eye of extinction. On a bright August day, I was campaigning for office at a county fair in southwestern Washington State. That day I was fulfilling the proud American tradition of walking around the fairgrounds, holding my bright blue sign on my shoulder, and shaking hands with my fellow citizens, a ritual as old as the republic. I was generally enjoying the day when I was surprised to see a trailer holding a ten-foot-long Bengal tiger. The beast was pacing back and forth, with only a glass wall separating this pinnacle of evolutionary predation from the fairgoers. He was a magnificent assemblage of power and beauty, and having never been really close to a tiger before, I was blown away with its low-slung gait, its striking color, and its quiet, but menacing, energy. It may have been confined in a trailer at a fairground, but twelve inches away from me, it was as powerful and imposing as any wild tiger to me.

Then all of a sudden, it stopped dead still, and its eyes focused right on me and my bright blue sign with a lethal intensity that made me feel like the prey that we humans may have been a millennium ago. It didn't move a muscle, and neither did I. He was transfixed with something about my sign, and I was transfixed by something in his eye that

had a deeper carnivore-spirit than I had ever been on the receiving end of before. This predator-prey standoff went on for a few moments, long enough for me to get the willies, even though I was safely behind three inches of Plexiglas. I knew then what Blake meant by the lines, "What immortal hand and eye / could frame thy fearful symmetry?"* In an instant, I had felt the power of thousands of generations of evolution, all leading up to the creation of a supreme force of nature, a perfect blend of power and beauty, whose stripes framed what may have been camouflaged in the jungle, but that made its very hunting essence into a piece of irresistible movable art in my mind's eye.

After those long and intense moments, when he finally released me from the grip of his laser stare, a terrible thought, worse than the genetically wired fears of predation I had just experienced, struck me: This beast could be vanquished from the wild in my lifetime. This beauty could be erased from the Earth's chalkboard by the careless forces of mankind cavalierly dispensing extinction without a thought to its permanence or the loss to the planet.

My second insight into extinction was a species closer to home for me, and came recently in my Congressional office, as I mounted a six-foot-long photograph I had taken of a field of magenta paintbrush flowers growing in an alpine meadow at Hurricane Ridge in the Olympic National Park. I was putting this photo up on my wall in part because they reminded me of the alpine flowers my mother had so loved when she and my father worked with a youth group restoring the alpine meadows on the broad slopes of Mount Rainier in the '70s. These particular paintbrush flowers were unique, their hue of magenta existing nowhere else on the planet except in the Olympic Mountains.

But as I put the picture up, I remembered the park ranger who came upon me as I was crouching down to take the picture. He told me that these little sprites could be extinct in a hundred years because the tree line was moving up rapidly due to global warming, and eventually there would be no sunny alpine meadows for these treasures to grow in.

As I stepped back to check the level of the photo on the wall, it was discomforting to know that there could come a day when these unique jewels were only known in photographs. But facts are stubborn things, and the flowers that were meant to remind me of my mother, now also reminded me of the pending extinction of so many unique species from climate change, and habitat loss. The picture of these alpine meadow flowers my mother loved deserved better than to just be a sad reminder of species lost and disappearing. They need to be an inspiration to do something about it.

*From "The Tiger," by William Blake, in Arthur Quiller-Couch, ed., Oxford Book of English Verse, lines 3–4.

KASSIE SIEGEL
CLIMATE CHANGE

"Solving the climate crisis will require real change—not changes around the edges. And change is hard, but incredibly exciting."

Climate Change

→ **Issue:** Greenhouse gases are shifting the planet's climate system, to the detriment of species that have evolved to fill particular niches in the Earth's many varied ecosystems.

→ **Impact:** The Intergovernmental Panel on Climate Change has said that climate change is likely to overshadow habitat loss and other threats to wildlife as the main driver of biodiversity loss in the future.

→ **Trend:** Arctic regions are being disproportionately impacted by climate change and associated higher levels of atmospheric warming.

Kassie Siegel

→ **Education:** JD from University of California, Berkeley, School of Law

→ **Nationality:** American

→ **Organizational Affiliation:** Center for Biological Diversity

→ **Years Working on Climate Change:** 15

→ **Honors:** Named one of California's ten most influential lawyers of the decade by the *Daily Journal* (2007), and named one of *California Lawyer*'s "Attorneys of the Year" (2007)

→ **Notable Accomplishments:** Author of the successful petition to list polar bears under the U.S. Endangered Species Act

KASSIE Siegel's passion to protect wild animals and wild places led her to make history when she persuaded the U.S. government to acknowledge for the first time that climate change was a threat to a wildlife species—the beloved Arctic icon, the polar bear.

Siegel's path to becoming a wildlife advocate started in the unlikely New Jersey suburbs where she grew up. Despite a lack of wild animals or wilderness expanses in her hometown, she was inspired by what she saw in pictures and documentaries, and sought out opportunities to explore nature. After going through college on a tennis athletic scholarship, she committed to fully immersing in nature, and moved to Alaska to be an apprentice raft guide. Three years of river rafting in one of the most beautiful natural environments in the world convinced her to return to the Lower 48 and go to law school to gain the skills and tools she would need to protect the outdoors she loved.

Right out of law school, Siegel joined two fellow students—Brent Plater and Brendan Cummings—to open the Berkeley, California, office of the Center for Biological Diversity. The three of them realized that climate change was going to be the biggest threat to wildlife in the future, but at that time, there was very little scientific information linking climate change to species declines. Cummings—who is not only Siegel's work partner, but also her life partner—came up with the idea of

using the U.S. Endangered Species Act of 1973 (ESA) to bring attention to the impact climate change would have on animal species.

A recent study had shown that the receding glaciers in Glacier Bay, Alaska, were threatening an endemic wolf spider that depended on the glaciers for survival. Siegel points out, "It was the most charming species—with these adorable hairy little legs. But after much debate we decided that a wolf spider would probably not be the ideal poster child for linking the threats of climate change to species loss." She and her colleagues went on to petition for ESA listings for the Kittlitz's Murrelet—a seabird also reliant on Alaskan glaciers—and two types of ocean corals disappearing as a result of increases in ocean temperatures and rising ocean acidity. But none of these efforts caught the attention of the media or public, and therefore failed to spur the government to link the species' imperilment to climate change.

But then, in 2004, two reports came out that gave Siegel and Cummings what they needed: a paper by leading polar bear biologists laying out what would happen to polar bears in a warming Arctic, and the Arctic Climate Impact Assessment. "We had been talking about polar bears the whole time, but there had been very little science done. Then these reports came out from highly respected sources saying that climate change was causing the Arctic ice to melt, and that if the Arctic ice melts, polar bears will go extinct. It connected all the dots perfectly."

With polar bears, Siegel and Cummings had found the iconic climate change species they had been searching for. With the two reports in hand, Siegel and Cummings wrote a science-based 170-page technical petition to list polar bears on the ESA. "I sent out press releases the night before we filed, and got up early the next morning to try to pitch the story to anyone who would listen. To my surprise, it was already posted online at a number of sites by the time I got to the office. By the middle of the day, the story was everywhere and we were making national and international news. The link between polar bears and climate change had clicked with the world, where no other species had been able to make that connection before."

Climate change—a shift in the Earth's climate system caused by the emission of greenhouse gases and other factors—is predicted to be the number one cause of loss of the planet's animal and plant species in the future. Greenhouse gases—specifically carbon dioxide, methane, nitrous oxide, and fluorinated

What You Should Know about Climate Change

→ Carbon dioxide emissions from the combustion of petroleum, coal, and natural gas are the leading source of greenhouse gas emissions from the United States.

→ Other sources of man-made greenhouse gases include gas from landfills, coal mines, agriculture, and oil and natural gas operations, as well as emissions from nitrogen fertilizers, burning fossil fuels, and certain industrial and waste management practices.

→ Effects of climate change include average surface warming of the planet, a rise in ocean acidity levels and sea level, increased frequency of temperature extremes, and increased intensity and frequency of weather events, such as droughts and tropical storms.

→ Polar animals dependent on ice for survival are already being impacted by climate change. This includes polar bears, penguins, seals, walruses, and tiny krill and copepods—small crustaceans that form the vital bottom of the food pyramid at the poles.

gases—are released into the atmosphere mainly from combustion of fossil fuels. Petroleum, coal, and natural gas account for the lion's share of human-caused greenhouse gas emissions in the United States and most developed countries. How different species will adapt or respond to climactic changes varies based on a number of factors, but species that have evolved to be dependent on narrower climatic habitat niches will face significant challenges to their survival. For example, ice-dependent species, such as polar bears, walruses, and penguins, are already being impacted by differences in the ice pack from climate change.

Polar bears in particular rely on the Arctic sea ice for hunting, locating mates, raising their young, and movement across long distances. Shrinking summer ice has led to sightings of malnourished polar bears and the first documented cases of polar bears drowning in open water while trying to swim between ice floes. The best available science is predicting that unless climate change is curbed or stopped, two-thirds of the world's polar bears—including all those in Alaska—will be gone in half a century or sooner.

In 2008, faced with mounting public concern for polar bears and pressure to protect the species, the U.S. government listed polar bears as threatened. *Newsweek* magazine ran a cover story on the polar bear listing, centered around Siegel and Cummings's strategy to use the polar bear as a poster child for the danger climate change poses to Earth's species. And while other species have since been proposed for listing on the ESA due to climate change—such as pikas, four ice-dependent seal species, the Pacific walrus, and two species of Northern Canadian reindeer—none have gotten the media and public attention that the polar bear did.

Siegel has since moved on to looking at other environmental regulations that could help address climate change. "We passed all these amazing laws in the '60s and '70s that should be tools for addressing climate change: the ESA, the Clean Air Act, the Clean Water Act, the National Environmental Policy Act, and

others. We need to convince the government to use these laws to curb greenhouse gas emissions," says Siegel. "Solving the climate crisis will require real change—not changes around the edges. And change is hard, but incredibly exciting."

Siegel also continues to fight in court, supporting the polar bear listing, which a long line of economically interested parties have tried to strike down. "When we started," she says, "we were focused on raising awareness and educating people that global warming was happening now—especially if you happened to be a polar bear. Now we are asking, what can the law do to help? The ESA is one great tool for addressing climate change, as it requires every U.S. federal agency to look at ways to reduce emissions so that they do not further harm federally protected polar bears.

"Like so many people, I've always loved polar bears," she continues. "When I graduated from college, my gift to myself was a framed print of polar bears." Siegel saw her first wild polar bear thirteen years later. "No matter how many nature films or photos I'd seen, I was still completely blown away by the magnificence and magic of the animal in its arctic environment. It exceeded anything I could have imagined," she remembers. "And while I know things aren't looking good for the polar bear, I firmly believe we can save it. And I'm committed to spending the rest of my life trying to make some small contribution to making this happen."

GRACE GE GABRIEL
WILDLIFE CONSUMPTION

"It is hard to get people incensed about what is happening if they don't even associate the killing of the animal with the product."

Wildlife Consumption

→ **Issue:** Human demand for wildlife and wildlife products jeopardizes populations and species when it exceeds sustainable levels.

→ **Impact:** Along with habitat loss, climate change, and invasive species, overexploitation of wildlife is considered one of the top threats to global biodiversity.

→ **Trend:** Globalization and worldwide economic growth have stimulated and expanded supply and demand for wildlife and products made from wildlife.

Grace Ge Gabriel

→ **Education:** Master's degree from the University of Utah

→ **Nationality:** Chinese American

→ **Organizational Affiliation:** International Fund for Animal Welfare

→ **Years Addressing Wildlife Consumption:** 15

→ **Books Published:** Contributor to *Mending the Web of Life—Traditional Medicine and Species Conservation*

→ **Notable Accomplishments:** Opened IFAW's office in China to conduct animal welfare campaigns; established the only government-certified raptor rehabilitation center in China; convinced China's largest online shopping site to ban sales of certain imperiled wildlife on their website; participated in the drafting of China's first animal welfare legislation

GRACE Ge Gabriel works in the country with possibly the highest demand on Earth for wildlife products. Her work has saved numerous animals—both common and rare—from horrific fates: Tibetan antelopes, tigers, elephants, birds of prey, sharks, rhinos, pangolins, freshwater turtles, saigas, and bears, just to name a few. And they all have one thing in common—they are being pushed toward extinction by human demand for the creatures themselves or their various body parts. That is why Gabriel's role in conservation is so crucial— she specializes in efforts to help the animal victims of the vast and devastating wildlife trade, and simultaneously works to curb the consumer demand that stimulates this trade in the most populous country in the world, China.

Gabriel grew up in China during a period of political turmoil. Her parents, both members of the intellectual class, were persecuted in various political movements. As a result, she became painfully aware of social prejudices and injustice at a young age. This awareness cultivated her empathy and compassion, particularly toward those that are defenseless, such as animals.

Her first face-to-face encounter with the brutal implications of consumer demand for wildlife products changed her life. In 1996, while working as a journalist for KSL-TV in the United States, she

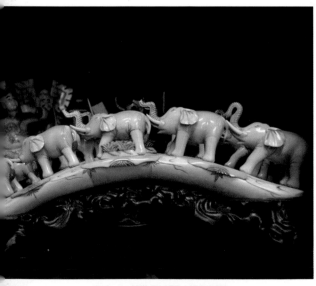

visited a bear bile farm in China as part of a story on the government-supported industry. She saw wild-caught bears in tiny cages, immobile for years while their bodily fluids were drained and sold as medicinal remedies. While witnessing bears rescued from this cruel trade taking their first steps at an International Fund for Animal Welfare (IFAW) bear sanctuary, Gabriel was so moved that she committed to turning her sorrow into action. She persuaded IFAW to allow her to open an office in Beijing, thereby becoming the first—and only—international animal welfare organization working in China.

One of Gabriel's first efforts in her new career was to design a campaign aimed at stopping the slaughter of Tibetan antelopes for the fine wool found on their underbellies. The wool is used to make luxury Shahtoosh shawls for wealthy Western consumers. Gabriel tackled the problem with a two-pronged approach: She helped build capacity for antipoaching patrols in China's Tibetan Plateau—the only place on Earth where wild Tibetan antelopes are found; then she launched consumer-awareness campaigns in Europe and the United States, where Shahtoosh shawls were being illegally traded. She also helped China draft a resolution to control Shahtoosh trade, which was later adopted by the countries to the Convention on International Trade in Endangered Species. As part of her outreach campaign, she successfully lobbied the U.S. government to list Tibetan antelopes as Endangered under the Endangered Species Act, thereby empowering the U.S. government for the first time to prosecute sellers and buyers of Shahtoosh shawls in the U.S. With this campaign, Gabriel had embarked on the first in a series of powerful efforts aimed at ending consumer demand for endangered species.

In the past quarter century, China's economic boom has created a swelling middle class with burgeoning consuming power. Combined with a consumerism culture and the increase of online trade, this buying power has increased pressure on wildlife

species—particularly those with a history of exploitation, such as elephants and tigers. To address this, Gabriel has initiated strategic consumer-awareness campaigns throughout China, trying to stop the demand side of the trade. "So long as there is a market for wildlife products, wild tigers and elephants will never be safe." Gabriel has a particular affinity for saving the tiger. Born at dusk in the Chinese Year of the Tiger, she grew up being told by her mother that she has the characteristics of a tiger. "My love for tigers—and all cats, for that matter—may have sprung from that connection," she says.

Getting attention on the demand side of the wildlife trade can be very challenging. Grace observes, "It is hard to get people incensed about what is happening if they don't even associate the killing of the animal with the product. For example, the Chinese word for *elephant ivory* translates as 'elephant teeth'—and people think the elephant teeth must fall out naturally. Or they believe the lies told by trade promoters that Shahtoosh wool can

be taken from the Tibetan antelope without killing it. There is a real disconnect between the product and suffering of the animal necessary to supply it."

"Additionally, an industry that promotes wildlife trade can always use cultural tradition as an excuse for exploitation." Grace believes that respect for nature and compassion for other beings are values that have a much longer history in China than the more recent trends of overexploiting. "Wars, foreign invasions and occupations, civil conflicts, and political movements have stripped away religious beliefs, basic trust between people, compassion and empathy, and a long-term view toward natural resources," said Gabriel. "Mass-marketing wildlife products in places like government-sanctioned tiger farms and bear bile farms is a recent development. They are not only inhumane, but they stimulate a black-market demand for products made from these endangered species in the wild. Polls already show that most Chinese do not support consumption of endangered species when they know where the product is coming from. We have found that once people know the truth about cruelly derived wildlife products, they willingly reject them."

In addition to demand-reduction campaigns, Gabriel investigates the wildlife markets in order to provide information to facilitate law enforcement and stricter wildlife policies. "You can go into Chinese markets and find cages stacked taller than me—filled with all kinds of animals being sold as pets, as food . . . whatever use the buyer might have for them. As far as eyes can see, basins filled with freshwater turtles, snakes, and lizards. Caged pangolins, raptors, and civets. Paws of bears or tigers still with fur on them. It's overwhelming to witness such immense cruelty and the depletion of biodiversity in the region," states Gabriel. "But there is still hope. I see progress all the time."

For example, a Chinese ad agency donated millions of dollars' worth of ad space in support of the IFAW campaign to reduce wildlife consumption. A local manager of the same ad agency specifically put a billboard at the entrance of China's largest ivory market in the city of Guangzhou, pleading for shoppers not to buy ivory. And in 2008, Gabriel scored a huge victory on behalf of animals when years of efforts by her and her staff got China's largest online shopping site, Taobao.com (which means "treasure hunt" in Chinese), to establish a strict policy banning all sale of elephant ivory, bear bile, tiger bones, shark fins, rhino horns, and turtle shells on their website.

Perhaps the accomplishment of which Gabriel is most proud is establishing the only government-certified raptor rehabilitation center in China. Hundreds of birds of prey—falcons, kestrels, owls, and many other species—are captured illegally from the wild in China and sold on the market for food or smuggled as exotic pets. Prior to the center's establishment, if any birds were lucky enough to be seized by authorities before leaving the country, there was nowhere to take them. After watching six confiscated birds die at one attempted release because they lacked proper medical care and conditioning, Gabriel set up the center on the campus of Beijing Normal University, providing a model rehabilitation and release program for confiscated

raptors. Since the center opened in 2001, more than three thousand raptor patients have been admitted, and more than 60 percent of them have been successfully released back into the wild.

Gabriel's pioneering work on behalf of animals has introduced an animal welfare and conservation ethic into modern China where it was almost entirely missing before. Her campaigns have helped to save some of the rarest animals on Earth by reaching out to millions of Chinese consumers, as well as consumers around the world, urging them to stop before they buy wildlife, or products made from wildlife. Says Gabriel, "When the buying stops, so will the killing. Until then, I'll keep doing my part every day."

JUDY ST. LEGER

WILDLIFE DISEASE

"My career is sort of like 'CSI' for wildlife."

Wildlife Disease

→ **Issue:** Emerging infectious diseases in wildlife that have recently surfaced in varying species, are thought to be driven by human environmental changes.

→ **Impact:** Wildlife diseases cause direct and indirect loss of populations and species and are a serious threat to wildlife, human health, and entire ecosystems.

→ **Trend:** There have been an increasing number of species affected by both known and unknown pathogens over the past few decades in terrestrial, freshwater, and marine habitats.

Judy St. Leger

→ **Education:** DVM from Cornell University

→ **Nationality:** American

→ **Organizational Affiliation:** SeaWorld Parks & Entertainment

→ **Years Working on Wildlife Disease:** 20

→ **Honors:** Distinguished Lecturer Award from CL Davis Foundation (2008)

→ **Notable Accomplishments:** SeaWorld & Busch Gardens Conservation Fund board member; City of San Diego Wetlands advisory board; former president of the International Association for Aquatic Medicine; associate editor for *Veterinary Pathology*; Oiled Wildlife Care Network scientific review board, board member for the C. L. Davis Foundation for Veterinary Pathology

"MY career is sort of like 'CSI' for wildlife," states veterinary pathologist Judy St. Leger. And like the detectives on the popular crime scene investigation TV shows, St. Leger doesn't just want to know how an offense occurs; she also wants to know why. In her work at SeaWorld, she has been able to turn her natural scientific curiosity and love of animals into a career studying wildlife die-offs in nature and then applying what she learns to conservation on behalf of dozens of species. "It sounds strange to think that examining animals that have died is important for modern conservation," she says. "But I work with biologists from around the world to investigate causes of death in wildlife." St.

Leger's focus is marine life in United States waters, but conservationists and students working on finding answers to wildlife mysteries on virtually every continent seek out her knowledge and advice.

Pathologists (scientists who study diseases and their causes), epidemiologists (scientists who study the factors that cause or encourage disease), and wildlife veterinarians all play key roles in the wildlife conservation field. Their skills can be even more crucial when a species' population numbers have already been compromised from factors such as habitat loss or overexploitation, and the animal is now facing an additional threat from a disease that leaves it vulnerable to extinction. Recent

wildlife disease outbreaks that have caused great concern in the conservation community include the spread of the Ebola virus among Critically Endangered gorillas, anthrax bacteria causing mass hippopotamus deaths in Queen Elizabeth National Park in Uganda, and devil facial tumor disease, which has caused devastating losses among Tasmanian devil populations in Australia. Similarly, fungal diseases have been linked to mass die-offs of amphibians, bats, and other pollinators. Without wildlife disease experts like St. Leger on hand to investigate these disasters, the die-offs would still be unexplained, with little opportunity to mitigate and manage the extent of the losses.

Finding answers to wildlife crises such as these in marine species is where St. Leger excels. "Exchange of information is key in determining causal factors in large-scale mortality events," she says. This is one reason she serves as editor for the journal *Veterinary Pathology*. "No one person can solve these disease epidemics alone—it takes all the resources, expertise, and information we can assemble."

St. Leger has been a compassionate animal lover since childhood. Her first real job involved cleaning kennels and assisting the veterinary staff in her hometown veterinary hospital. She was so impressed by the knowledge and compassion of the vets for whom she worked that she eventually attended veterinary school and returned to that same hospital to practice. "My role had changed," she says, "but the desire I had to aid each and every animal that came in was still the same."

As St. Leger worked, she saw that birds, reptiles, and other, more uncommon species were much less understood than dogs and cats. She began to transfer the knowledge she had gained with domestic animals to the more exotic species—pets at the clinic and exhibit animals at the local zoo. But no matter how comparable the species, wild animals were different—and she set out to find out how and why. "That's what led me to pathology," she explains. "If I could understand the health concerns of wildlife, I could make a large-scale difference."

This path brought St. Leger to SeaWorld, where she could use her skills, knowledge, and passion to understand how best to help lesser-studied animals. "It has been a dream job for me," she enthuses. "I work closely with some of the best marine mammal vets in the world, yet I have the ability to expand my work to the population level. There has been an increasing understanding among scientists that health concerns in wildlife reflect issues in the environment."

For example, in 2004 St. Leger investigated the deaths of hundreds of pelicans found off course and starving in different parts of North America. No one knew why this was happening, and the possibility of some strange new disease affecting pelicans seemed likely. Hundreds of these dazed, weak, and disoriented birds ended up at SeaWorld for rehabilitation after rescue. After months of work, St. Leger and her colleagues were able to rule out what had originally been thought to be the leading disease suspects: red tide–linked poisoning or a viral epidemic. Ultimately, St. Leger concluded, "It was likely a food shortage during a high chick-producing season, which might have been a onetime fluke. But the thing is that there's

What You Should Know about Wildlife Disease

→ Different diseases can pass from humans to wildlife, from one species of wildlife to another, and from wildlife to humans.

→ Factors such as pollution, introduction of invasive species, human encroachment into wildlife habitat, and increased presence and densities of domestic animals have been shown to play a part in disease emergence and proliferation.

→ Emerging diseases have been detected in species population declines on a massive scale worldwide, including amphibians, coral, bats, fish, birds, seals, and bees.

→ Globalization of agriculture and commerce plays a large role in the spread of emerging diseases. Pathogens "hitchhike" into new and nonresistant populations spreading rapidly around the world.

→ Extreme weather conditions, such as drought or intense rains, brought on by climate change, can exacerbate disease epidemics in wildlife populations.

still something unusual going on. There have been mass strandings more regularly, with quite a variety of avian species. What we learned from the 2004 pelican incidents can hopefully be applied to these new events, and move us faster toward identifying a cause of, and solution to, future die-offs."

One thing that St. Leger has learned from her work is that solving the mysteries surrounding animal deaths often goes much further than simply identifying the disease agent: investigations into the health of wildlife also involves looking at human and environmental effects on these species. "Humans and our influence are such a force on the natural world now that it is almost impossible to separate wildlife deaths from the anthropological causes and catalysts that feed into the problem." As a result, St. Leger must not only look for natural diseases in wildlife, but she

also has the additional complication of sorting out the man-made factors causing or contributing to wildlife deaths. In a marine environment this includes such things as drowning in fishing nets, ship strikes, pollution, or reduced food availability from overfishing by humans.

St. Leger sees hundreds of animals that have had negative interactions with these human influences. "In 2008 I worked with a team to document the damage due to abandoned fishing gear on turtles, birds, dolphins, sea lions, and other marine species. It's a huge problem resulting in the deaths of thousands and thousands of sea animals," observes St. Leger, "but unless people are aware of the problem, it won't improve." That study led to new programs designed to clean up coastal areas to prevent entanglement of more animals. This project is still active today as part of the programs of the SeaDoc Society. St. Leger is also a member of the scientific review board for the Oiled Wildlife Care Network, a California statewide cooperative that is recognized as a world leader in oil spill response, rehabilitation of oiled animals, and research into the best methods for the successful return of rehabbed animals to the wild.

St. Leger's job has some surprising moments, like the time she was asked to find out why a satellite tracking tag attached to a gray whale had stopped moving—it usually means just one thing, and St. Leger wasn't looking forward to finding that the whale had died. She traveled to the location of the signal in Mexico and ended up in a

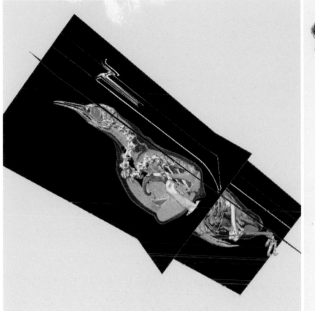
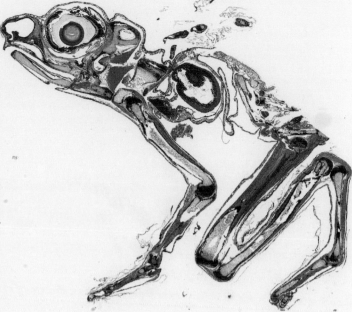

remote fishing village. After searching the beach for the body of the whale for hours, she began to ask around in broken Spanish, "¿Dónde está la ballena?" After a few exchanges, she understood that what she was looking for was at the village market. And sure enough, at the market, there was the satellite tag, but no whale. It turns out, the whale had snagged the tag on a fisherman's net—the whale swam away, but the tag remained. The fisherman figured someone would come looking, so he dropped off the tag at the market. "That was one of the best necropsies I never had to perform!" says St. Leger.

St. Leger is currently investigating health concerns of free-ranging killer whales off the Pacific Coast. When a young whale stranded in Santa Barbara, California, in 2008, St. Leger joined the team to figure out why. It was discovered that the calf died from Salmonella—a genus of bacteria that sickens people as well. Scientists rarely get the chance to examine marine mammal deaths in the wild since most marine animals never make it to shore. St. Leger was able to apply this information and put it into context with health irregularities occurring in open ocean pods. So while one animal doesn't necessarily tell the whole story, St. Leger has been able to use individuals to examine what is happening to larger populations as more information becomes available.

"There are many roles one can play in conservation—from protecting habitat to protecting individual animals." Says St. Leger, "My work focuses on keeping track of the health of many species. If I do my job well, I can help others to understand the challenges that wild animals face. From there we can figure out what needs to be done to help them survive."

WANGARI MAATHAI
HABITAT LOSS

"We need to rethink our concept of peace and security. We need to look at the way we manage and share our resources. Only then do we have hope."

FAST FACTS

Habitat Loss

→ **Issue:** Activities such as resource extraction, conversion of land for agriculture and grazing, and human encroachment, as well as pollution and fragmentation from roads and development, result in the loss of essential habitat for wildlife.

→ **Impact:** All species have certain food, water, and shelter requirements. The greater the loss or degradation of these basic necessities, the poorer the quality and quantity of life the habitat can sustain.

→ **Trend:** While the rate of growth of the human population is projected to steadily decline in the future, the human population itself will continue to expand, requiring more resources and space.

Wangari Maathai

→ **Education:** PhD from the University of Nairobi, Kenya

→ **Nationality:** Kenyan

→ **Organizational Affiliation:** The Green Belt Movement

→ **Years Working on Habitat Loss:** 35+

→ **Honors:** Named by *Time* magazine as one of the 100 Most Influential People in the World (2005); Nobel Peace Prize (2004); the Conservation Scientist Award (2004); Excellence Award from the Kenyan Community Abroad (2001); Golden Ark Award (1994); Jane Adams Leadership Award (1993), Edinburgh Medal (1993); Goldman Environmental Prize (1991); Windstar Award for the Environment (1988); numerous other awards and honors

→ **Books Published:** *Unbowed: A Memoir* (autobiography); *Replenishing the Earth: Spiritual Values for Healing Ourselves and the World*; *The Challenge for Africa*; *The Green Belt Movement: Sharing the Approach and the Experience*; coauthored several other books

→ **Notable Accomplishments:** The first woman in East and Central Africa to earn a doctorate degree; chaired the department of veterinary anatomy at the University of Nairobi; former chair of the National Council of Women of Kenya; cochair of the Jubilee 2000 Africa Campaign; appointed by Kenya's president as assistant minister for environment, natural resources, and wildlife in Kenya's ninth parliament; United Nations Messenger of Peace, with a special focus on the environment and climate change; first African woman and first environmental activist to win a Nobel Peace Prize

What You Should Know about Habitat Loss

→ Habitat loss is identified as the primary threat to 85 percent of species listed as Endangered or Threatened on the IUCN Red List.

→ The human population is expected to reach 7 billion in 2012 and somewhere between 8 billion and 10.5 billion by 2050, requiring more already scarce resources.

→ In 2010, just over 12 percent of the world's land and less than 1 percent of the world's oceans qualified as protected areas.

→ The Ramsar Convention on Wetlands of International Importance, the Convention on Biological Diversity, the Millennium Development Declaration, and the World Heritage Convention are just a few of the international agreements that are attempting to address the threat of habitat loss.

BORN and raised in one of the most diverse and abundant wildlife regions in the world, activist and conservationist Wangari Maathai knows that quality of life in Africa is dependent on the quality of the environment. In 2004, when she became the first African woman to win the Nobel Peace Prize, Maathai spoke of her early connection to the natural world. "I would visit a stream next to our home to fetch water for my mother. I would drink water straight from the stream. Playing among the arrowroots, I tried in vain to pick up the strands of frogs' eggs, believing they were beads." Within her lifetime, however, environmental degradation of the planet has become readily apparent, and as Maathai grew older, things changed. "I witnessed forests being cleared and replaced by commercial plantations, which destroyed local biodiversity and the capacity of forests to conserve water," she says. Her childhood stream dried up, and women from her village had to walk much farther to gather water and firewood. Both extremes of Maathai's personal experiences helped form her passion for a healthy planet—a passion that has led her to worldwide recognition as a committed environmentalist working to preserve a rapidly changing world.

In their relatively short time on Earth, humans have modified more than 50 percent of the land on the planet—usually resulting in less-favorable conditions for other species. Approximately 35 percent of the world's coral reefs and 50 percent of mangrove habitats, two of the most important ecosystems for ocean productivity, are in critical condition or already destroyed. Human population is expanding most rapidly in less-developed regions, and more people need more resources. Combine that with the demands the world economy places on Africa's resources as well, and that equates to less food, forests, and space for the animals that share the land and water. Herbivores, like elephants, giraffes, and hippos, need large land areas with plenty of vegetation to eat and water to drink, but they now have fragmented ranges, with heavy poaching for ivory, meat, hair, and hides. Primates, antelope, birds, and scores of other animals rely on healthy, intact forests for survival; but forests are being cut down, either tree by tree to satisfy a growing demand for wood for cooking and heating, or from large-scale logging and clearing for agriculture. Predators such as leopards, lions, and hyenas are persecuted for their threat to livestock.

The Earth has enormous capacity for sustaining life. From the time life is first thought to have appeared on our planet, about 3 billion years ago, to now, life has diversified and coexists in the most amazing and unique ways. Maathai grew up fascinated by nature and appreciative that everything has a place and a value in the ecosystem. The complexity of the enormous variety and number of species in Africa is not unique, but still astounding. That giraffes, the tallest land animals, benefit from one of the smallest, the dung beetle, through the services of waste removal and nutrient recycling it provides, is testament to the often obscure interactions of species. The symbiosis of wasps and figs, and the birds and other animals that eventually eat this fruit, move to new locations, and disperse the seeds to start the process all over again, is a long, evolved, and essential survival strategy not exceptional in nature. Losing some particular aspect, one type of tree, one species, one location, may prevent an entire progression of events from happening. In fact, each species of fig is pollinated by just one particular species of wasp. And it is only after an

impregnated female wasp burrows out of the fig that the fruit begins to ripen, providing nutritious food for multitudes of birds and other animals.

Habitat loss leads to the demise of these complex interactions and connections needed to sustain an ecosystem. And humans have not just consumed more; they have rapidly forced change in the way other organisms must live; other life on the planet must now adapt quickly or die. Many changes simply remove the options for survival. When migration corridors are eliminated, wildlife has nowhere else to go. When access to seasonal food and water supplies is cut off, animals often have no other course of action than to "steal" from their human neighbors. Conflict, retaliation, and losses result on both sides of the "fence." Consequently, species populations, once wide-ranging and socially connected, are fragmented and genetically limited in much of the world today.

Humans also want what the Earth contains, not just what's on top. Mining operations for coal and minerals such as gold and diamonds create harmful side effects. Mining has been shown to be one of the most environmentally destructive operations on Earth. Mountains are moved, pits are dug, rock is dynamited, mercury and cyanide are used to extract, and methane is released in just some of the different mining processes. Add to all that the chemical and pesticide use, which persists in the environment for decades; road building through pristine areas; electronic, plastic, and hazardous waste disposal; water and air pollution; draining of wetlands; and nutrient overload, which places additional strain on the planet, and you have a quickly eroding natural environment.

But luckily the planet has heroes such as Maathai, who are committed to reversing these trends. Maathai knows that her ancestors and those of most Africans valued the mountains for their watershed, the forests for their bounty, and the animals for their ecosystem role in supporting life on the planet—including humans. She has based much of her life's work on the belief that individual actions of improving the environment—of planting a tree, or protecting a forest—are empowering. Maathai set this principle in motion as early as the mid-1970s when she proposed a program employing Kenyans—and in particular, women—to plant trees to restore degraded habitat. It was called Envirocare, and the idea led to the planting of the first "green belt." That initiative began the successful and incredibly powerful ideals of the Green Belt Movement, still based today in Nairobi, Kenya. "Because many of the problems women faced were due to environmental degradation, it was easy to identify tree planting as a doable activity, because it's practical, requires virtually no technology, and it is easy to teach to others and replicate," states Maathai. Since the start of the organization in 1977, more than 40 million trees have been planted and thirty thousand women have been given jobs and training that help them provide for their families while also improving the environment.

Throughout her life Maathai has been an inspiration to the women—and men—of Africa by standing up and speaking out for both humans and wildlife, often placing herself in the middle of controversy. Even when faced with political persecution, she remained "unbowed," which is also the appropriately named title of her autobiography, published in 2007. Maathai was awarded the Nobel Peace Prize in 2004 for her efforts in environmental sustainability, democracy, and peace. "We need to rethink our concept of peace and security," she contends. "We need to look at the way we manage and share our resources. Only then do we have hope." Her message connecting peace, security, welfare, and the environment has resonated with the world.

Maathai's simple tree-planting strategy has also become a symbol for activism, for empowerment, and for peaceful coexistence, with fellow humans and the environment. In 2009, the United Nations showed their support for Maathai's philosophy and actions, and named her a Messenger for Peace, joining the exceptional company of Jane Goodall, Michael Douglass, and Stevie Wonder, among others.

Maathai's philosophy to halt habitat loss through restoration, create a sustainable ethic, and accept responsibility to do one's part is paramount in turning around the loss of habitat for wildlife and for a healthy human existence. Maathai is committed to creating a future for Africa and the world where children are not deprived of drinking from clean, flowing streams or playing with the creatures found within—like the frogs and their pearl-like eggs she used to poke as a child.

SYLVIA EARLE
OCEAN DEGRADATION

"With knowing comes caring, and
with caring, there is hope that
we will find an enduring place for
ourselves within the natural systems
that sustain us."

Ocean Degradation

→ **Issue:** It was once thought the oceans could never be degraded or over-exploited due to their vastness. This has proven false.

→ **Impact:** Over-fishing, pollution, oil spills, climate change, nitrogen runoff, shipping, acidification and costal development, among other factors, all have significant impacts on ocean health, productivity and ultimately, life on this planet.

→ **Trend:** It is estimated that less than 4 percent of ocean area is unaffected by at least some detrimental anthropogenic effects. With the Earth's population continuing to increase, and demand for ocean resources continuing to expand, the trend is currently negative for most ocean environments.

Sylvia Earle

→ **Education:** PhD from Duke University; 20 honorary degrees

→ **Nationality:** American

→ **Organizational Affiliation:** National Geographic; SEAlliance; Harte Research Institute

→ **Years Addressing Ocean Degradation:** 40

→ **Honors:** More than 100 national and international honors including: The Royal Geographic Society's Gold Medal (2011); The TED Prize (2009); The National Women's Hall of Fame (2000); Library of Congress Living Legend (2000); Time Magazine Hero for the Planet (1998); The Explorer's Club Medal (1996); The Netherlands Order of the Golden Ark (1981).

→ **Books Published:** Over 180 publications on marine science, technology and conservation, including *Sea Change: A Message of the Oceans; Exploring the Deep Frontier; Dive; Wild Ocean; National Geographic Illustrated Atlas of the Ocean;* and *The World is Blue.*

→ **Notable Accomplishments:** Chief scientist for U.S. National Oceanic and Atmospheric Administration from 1990–1992; National Geographic explorer-in-residence 1998-present; founded Deep Ocean Exploration and Research in 1992; led more than 60 marine expeditions; holds the depth record for a solo submersible vehicle dive at 1000 meters

NO human has been deeper under the ocean's surface alone than Sylvia Earle. That fact symbolizes the spirit, love of nature, and courage in facing the unknown that has marked Earle's long and exciting career. Her exploration of, and concern for, the environment, whether at the incredible depth of 1,250 feet underwater in a pressurized suit or as Chief Scientist for the National Oceanic and Atmospheric Administration, has been a passion since Earle was a child. "Both of my parents nurtured my fascination of the outdoors and taught me to respect and protect nature, even what I didn't yet understand. I don't think they realized the extent to which I'd take those lessons!"

During college, Earle specialized in botany, as she feels that is the best foundation for understanding complex living systems. For her graduate degree in the mid-1960s, she created an exhaustive study and index of marine vegetation in the Gulf of

Mexico. And Earle's still adding to that information, but the environment has changed considerably since then. "The issues are more numerous now—from plastic debris which wasn't even around when I first began diving, to trawling, shark fining, and loss of mangroves and other fish nurseries. The ocean is resilient, but there are limits to what we can put in—and take out—without harmful consequences both to the ocean—and to us."

The ocean environment is influential, providing often unacknowledged benefits to humans and all life on Earth. It is the greatest determining factor in climate trends due to its enormous heat trapping and redistribution capability—a thousand times greater than the atmosphere. Oceans also store about 90 percent of the world's carbon and transports 90 percent of goods in trade. The wonder and awe that the ocean and its creatures generate is something Earle wants everyone to experience. Many people have never seen a live swordfish or cuttlefish and she believes once you realize how magnificent and important these animals are, you'll be more likely to care about conserving them for the future.

Earle sees the blue fin tuna as representative of both the extraordinary life within the oceans and its crises. Blue fin tuna can grow to more than 1,000 pounds, migrating thousands of miles before returning to their natal waters to spawn. The blue fin tuna is actually warm blooded—they regulate their body temperature—which allows them greater range and speed. Earle has enormous

What You Should Know About the Oceans

→ Many fish and other sea creatures taken for food have declined by 90 percent since 1950. Phytoplankton, the source of most of the oxygen in the atmosphere has declined by 40 percent.

→ About half of shallow coral reefs globally have disappeared or are in a state of serious decline since the middle of the 20th century. In the Caribbean, 80 percent are gone. Their loss affects thousands of species, including humans.

→ The blue whale, an ocean inhabitant, is the largest animal to have ever lived.

→ Coastal and marine environments support an estimated 13 million jobs for workers in just the United States alone.

→ The ocean produces more oxygen than all the worlds forests combined.

respect for these magnificent fish. "These incredible fish can live twenty-five years, swim at fifty miles per hour, and are key predators of the ocean. Yet their populations have declined by 90 percent due to over fishing." Despite their precipitous population crash, the international community has declined to increase protections for the species. At the 2010 meeting of the Convention on International Trade in Endangered Species of Wild Fauna and Flora, or CITES, with clear evidence of trade-related declines, proposals for increased safeguards against unsustainable take of blue fin tuna were all defeated.

Soon after this decision, the massive oil spill in the Gulf of Mexico affected one of the blue fin tuna's two known Atlantic breeding habitats. "The oil spill is a tragedy for the blue fin tuna and the entire Gulf ecosystem. The Gulf of Mexico will never be the same—for the people nor its aquatic life. Nature has an amazing capacity for healing and it could do so in time, but we must allow it to recover and not continue to add challenge after challenge." Earle is considered an expert on the effects of oil spills and has been called upon to assist following many of the world's major spills including those in the Persian Gulf, Alaska, and the Gulf of Mexico. In this role, Earle works to determine how to best help mend the marine environment after these disasters.

Oceans cover approximately 70 percent of the Earth's surface, yet less than 1 percent is protected from damaging practices. Many people still believe the oceans are so vast and deep, humans can't really have an effect on them. However, the methods humans have used to extract resources from the ocean have by most accounts been destructive; not sustainable. Trawlers and dragnets scrape the ocean floor like a forest clearcut, leaving devastation behind, even though only one species may be targeted. Long lines with miles of baited open hooks catch not just the intended species, but thousands of other animals as well—often turtles and birds. Called by-catch,

it's a horrific waste of life. The contaminants humans have dumped into the oceans, either purposely or accidently, from sewage and garbage to plastics and oil, do not disappear—they remain, affecting the marine wildlife—and humans themselves. "It's not just about the blue fin tuna, although that would be enough for me," says Earle. "I realize most people need a personal reason to care; well that's there too."

Earle has inspired thousands of people through books too numerous to mention, lectures in more than sixty countries, amazing discoveries, incredible exploration, and her unquenchable passion for the 97 percent of the water on Earth we call ocean. Earle reminds people that without the oceans, which shape climate, generate most of the oxygen in the atmosphere, and store massive amounts of CO_2, there would be no life on this planet. Earle remains optimistic. "Luckily, our ability to influence the marine environment goes both ways—we still have the opportunity to turn it around. With knowing comes caring, and with caring, there is hope that we will find an enduring place for ourselves within the natural systems that sustain us."

EDGARDO GRIFFITH
AMPHIBIAN DECLINE

"I realized how bad this really was when after a few years I went back to the same cloud forest where I first fell in love with amphibians and I was not able to find anything—nothing. All the creatures I fell in love with were just gone."

Amphibian Decline

→ **Issue:** Amphibians are facing the highest risk of extinction any group of animals has faced since the extinction of dinosaurs. Pollution, habitat loss, disease, and introduced species are a few of the factors negatively affecting them.

→ **Impact:** Scientists estimate that fully one-third to one-half of all amphibian species are currently threatened with extinction. More than 160 species have been classified as Extinct in just the last 20 years.

→ **Trend:** As a class of animals, numbers and species are disappearing increasingly rapidly since the 1980s.

Edgardo Griffith

→ **Education:** Bachelor of science in zoology from the University of Panama

→ **Nationality:** Panamanian

→ **Organizational Affiliation:** El Valle Amphibian Conservation Center and the Houston Zoo, Smithsonian Tropical Research Institute

→ **Years Working on Addressing Amphibian Decline:** 12

→ **Honors:** Association of Zoos and Aquariums (AZA) Top Honors Award for International Conservation Project (2010); Zoo Conservation Outreach Group Scholarship for Latin Americans recipient (2007).

→ **Notable Accomplishments:** Established and directs the El Valle Amphibian Conservation Center; consultant with the Panama Amphibian Rescue Center

EDGARDO Griffith was well on his way to a degree in microbiology and parasitology when he spent three days in October 2000 in Santa Fe National Park cloud forest high in the mountains of western Panama. He was introduced to so many species of amphibians and the pristine woods and streams they inhabited that he immediately decided to change his major to zoology, just to be able to work with frogs, toads, salamanders, newts, and caecilians, a lesser-known type of wormlike amphibian. "It was incredible—seeing such a variety of different species was simply fascinating—that trip changed my life forever," states Griffith. Before this trip, he had learned about a fungus that was spreading and destroying amphibian populations worldwide. Knowledge that these unique creatures could be facing global extinction only confirmed his decision.

Most amphibians have thin, moist, porous skin that helps them breathe, something not found elsewhere in the animal kingdom, and about 70 percent switch from gills to lungs as they move to a more terrestrial life—also a unique trait. Amphibians have long been considered an "indicator species"—bringing early attention to environmental change or degradation that may soon affect other species.

Being that most amphibians need both land and water to complete their life cycle, they are particularly vulnerable. Threats to amphibians today include habitat loss, pollution, toxic chemicals, over-collection from the wild, and introduced competing species. Scientists have also been studying a mysterious disease that began killing off entire amphibian populations more than forty years ago and has attacked on at least four continents. It is now known that the deadly agent is a chytrid fungus, called *Batrachochytrium dendrobatidis*. It has spread around the world, but is traced back to frogs imported by the thousands from South Africa, originally for medical uses. Between one-third and one-half of all six thousand known species of frogs worldwide have already been affected and are in danger of extinction due to a combination of threats, led by the chytrid fungus.

The mystery of amphibian decline was first reported in 1966 with a stunning bright, shiny, orange toad. The species, called the *golden toad*, was only found in Costa Rica's Monteverde Cloud Forest Preserve, a high-altitude haven for amphibians. While scientists were studying this unique little toad, the population suddenly crashed. May 1989 was the last time a golden toad was seen—one solitary male. None have been found since, and the International Union for the Conservation of Nature has declared the species extinct. Since then, scientists have attributed the loss of the golden toad to a variety of factors, including climate change (the toad disappeared during the driest period in these mountains' recorded history), pollution, and the chytrid fungus.

In a sadly similar situation within the biologically diverse Central American country of Panama, scientists had already conducted amphibian surveys within Omar Torrijos National Park, located in El Copé, between 1998 and 2004 and recorded sixty-three species of amphibians prior to the appearance of the chytrid fungus. The fungus was detected in 2004, so this park lent itself well to a before-and-after evaluation. When the Smithsonian

What You Should Know about Amphibian Decline

→ Amphibians have existed on Earth for more than 300 million years, yet scientists are discovering new species almost as fast as some are going extinct.

→ Almost 90 percent of all amphibians are frogs or toads.

→ Due to amphibians' reliance on both water and terrestrial environments, and their extremely permeable skin, they are among the first animals to be affected by worsening environmental conditions.

→ The largest amphibian is the Chinese giant salamander, which can grow to the size of a person. The most unusual may be the olm, a cave-dwelling, sightless salamander who locates food by smell and sensing electromagnetic fields. It has been shown to survive ten years without eating.

→ Due to their sensitive and porous skin, frogs protect themselves by producing chemicals with antibacterial properties. These chemicals have been used to help fight antibiotic-resistant infections in humans.

Tropical Research Institute, with which Griffith is associated, went back into the field to assess the damage, twenty-five of the sixty-three species had already disappeared from the region, while nine more species had declined by at least 85 percent. Since 2004, none of the amphibians have reappeared, and it was at that point that Griffith decided to look more closely at this amphibian devastation.

As reports of chytrid fatalities began pouring in, many scientists and conservationists began to realize these amphibian species could not be saved in the wild before succumbing to chytrid—the fungus was too aggressive and too complete in its destruction. Sponsored by the Houston Zoo as well as other zoological institutions, the concept for the El Valle Amphibian Conservation Center in Panama was designed in order to provide an *ex-situ* (out of its wild habitat) refuge for some of the most endangered species of amphibians in the region including seven found nowhere else in the world.

Griffith, with a zoology degree from the University of Panama in hand and a fire to save amphibians in his heart, was named director of the center. Construction of a facility began in August 2005; however, the chytrid fungus arrived in El Valle in December of the same year. Before the buildings were complete, Griffith began finding dead frogs in nearby streams in large numbers. "We had no place to house our treasured jewels. I contacted the owner of the local Hotel Campestre and worked out a deal with him and the manager. Two rooms were rented to house rescued frogs and four more to accommodate all the volunteers who wanted to help collect and care for them." After receiving the proper government permits, volunteers, under Griffith's direction, began collecting frogs.

This unique solution, Griffith's "Frog Hotel" was featured on the front page of the *Washington Post*, in *National Geographic* magazine, and on the BBC. For a full year, Griffith and his team cared for the amphibians at the Frog Hotel. Finally, in May 2007 the frogs were able to be moved to their newly constructed facility. The team had now completed the first phase of the project—rescuing endangered Panamanian amphibians from the wild. The daily work, however, caring for more than five hundred frogs and collecting food for them every day and night, was constant. "It takes thousands of insects and other invertebrates to keep these frogs healthy," says Griffith. "But what is overwhelming is to look at some of the animals we have and know they are representing the last living individuals of their species, and they are now under our care. Any amount of effort is uncontested."

Frogs played a significant role in Griffith's meeting his future wife, Heidi, as he was working in El Copé, where he had been assisting with the frog surveys and Heidi was a Peace Corps volunteer. "The fact that I met my wife was 100 percent due to the frogs. On our first date I took her to see a population of amphibians I had been studying; she got hooked—and the rest is a story still being written by myself, Heidi, and the frogs."

In Panama and around the world, zoos, aquariums, and botanical gardens have stepped up to the plate to save amphibians by providing expertise, funding, training, facilities, and resources. States Griffith, "Zoological facilities have been the only reason why we are able to do what we do. They are today often the sole institutions that have the capa-

bility of caring for and successfully breeding some of the last representatives of over one hundred species of amphibians."

No one knows for sure how this crisis, called the greatest extinction event since the dinosaurs, will unfold. As of 2010, the IUCN Red List, which incorporates the Global Amphibian Assessment and subsequent updates, lists 486 amphibian species as "Critically Endangered." Griffith recalls, "I realized how bad this really was when after a few years I went back to the same cloud forest where I first fell in love with amphibians and I was not able to find anything—nothing. All the creatures I fell in love with were just gone. That was when I knew how important the work we are doing is."

STEVE GALSTER
WILDLIFE TRADE

"No one knows exactly how much the illegal wildlife trade is worth. Estimates go as high as $20 billion annually, and higher. But even with those kinds of numbers, I believe everyone is underestimating how big this trade is."

Wildlife Trade

→ **Issue:** Illegal trafficking in wildlife is a vast, illicit trade with huge impact on a wide number of species ranging from common to critically endangered.

→ **Impact:** Poaching and collection for wildlife trade is the leading threat driving species such as elephants, rhinos, pangolins, and seahorses toward extinction.

→ **Trend:** As an illegal trade, wildlife trafficking is believed to be eclipsed in scope and scale only by drugs and guns.

Steve Galster

→ **Education:** Master's degree in international security, George Washington University

→ **Nationality:** American

→ **Organizational Affiliation:** FREELAND

→ **Years Working on Addressing Wildlife Trade:** 21

→ **Honors:** Grinnell College Alumni Award (2009)

→ **Books Published:** *US Policy toward Afghanistan*

→ **Notable Accomplishments:** Founded Global Survival Network; cofounded WildAid; cofounded Phoenix Fund (Russia); founder of FREELAND organization; chief of party for the Association of Southeast Asian Nations' Wildlife Enforcement Network (ASEAN-WEN) support program; featured on CNN's *Planet in Peril* series; host of Animal Planet UK documentary series *Crime Scene Wild*; host of National Geographic TV's *Crimes against Nature*

STEVE Galster became a wildlife crusader through an unorthodox yet effective route: he was able to segue years of investigative and analytic work on militias around the world into a highly successful career bringing down international wildlife trade smugglers.

"I was doing very exciting work analyzing insurgency and counterinsurgency efforts in Afghanistan," Galster recalls, "dissecting black-market operations that were moving drugs, guns, and other illicit goods. But at the same time I was frustrated that so much of what I was working on were issues tied to important human-rights, and yet I had no control over follow-up. It was maddening to not see enough progress being made."

So in 1991, when the Environmental Investigation Agency (EIA) called him and asked him to look at cross-border African black-markets trafficking in both arms and wildlife, he took the opportunity as a chance to try something new. What he found was a thriving illegal trade in elephant ivory and rhino horns in southern Africa. He reported back what he discovered to EIA, and much to his surprise, he was able to see his recommendations turned into action less than a year later at a global forum for protecting wildlife from unsustainable trade.

"I had always been a wildlife lover," Galster says. "EIA liked my first analysis and saw the connections from my previous experiences, so I started investigating more countries—like Zambia and Mozambique, not only working with EIA but also helping these governments better understand the wildlife trade that was happening within their own borders. It just evolved from there. Next thing I knew I was working with undercover police, posing as a South African rhino horn dealer in Zambia and Zimbabwe, trying to get inside and understand this horrific trade."

Through his undercover investigations and research, Galster found that the illegal wildlife trade in products like elephant ivory and rhino horns was linked to the financing of militia forces in war-torn African nations. And the more he investigated, the more nefarious a business he discovered, including ties to highly organized crime syndicates trafficking in wildlife and wildlife products, such as sturgeon caviar, bear bile, butterflies, shark fins, and tropical orchids.

"No one knows exactly how much the illegal wildlife trade is worth. Estimates go as high as $20 billion annually, and higher. But even with those kinds of numbers, I believe everyone is underestimating how big the trade is. I have never worked with a government that is detecting more than 5 percent of what is actually going on."

The sale of wildlife goods happens all over the globe—including in the United States. A 2008 investigation by the International Fund for Animal Welfare tracked nearly two hundred open buyer-seller online platforms in eleven different countries over six weeks. During that short period, they found more than seven thousand endangered species and parts for sale, the majority of which were elephant ivory products sold on U.S. websites. Other animals and

animal products found in the investigation included exotic birds, primates, big cats, and reptiles.

Galster was one of the visionaries behind the development of "Department Tiger," also known as "Operation Amba" in the Russian Far East. To combat this unsustainable trade, Galster became a driving force in launching the Association of Southeast Asian Nations' Wildlife Enforcement Network—better known as ASEAN-WEN. Because of this collective of ten Southeast Asian countries, there is a commitment to addressing wildlife trade cooperatively in the region, something that has resulted in more wildlife trade busts and less flora and fauna leaving the area.

In 1999, Galster joined with three colleagues to found WildAid, an organization devoted to ending illegal trade in wildlife. For years Galster worked through WildAid to combat illicit wildlife trade via a combination of public outreach and enforcement efforts, with a focus on Southeast Asia. However, he always maintained an interest in human rights. Then in 2006, WildAid split into two organizations with complementary but different focuses, and Galster took this opportunity to bridge the wildlife conservation work of WildAid with the human rights field by eventually creating the organization FREELAND.

"While investigating Siberian tiger skin traffickers in Russia, I saw that these criminals were the same people trafficking in humans. When I handed over intelligence on the wildlife trade, I saw an indifference to the trade in women that was going on at the same time. So I came back and knew I had to expand my focus to include human trafficking."

Under Galster's leadership, a strong FREELAND team now engages in protected area training programs, investigations trainings, alternative livelihoods initiatives, prosecution support, and public awareness campaigns addressing consumer demand for wildlife products and stopping human trafficking.

With his charismatic persona and clear passion for his profession, Galster has been a natural magnet for media attention. His work was highlighted in the 2007 CNN series *Planet in Peril*. He also hosted Animal Planet's *Crime Scene Wild* series, and is prominently featured in the National Geographic television series *Crimes against Nature*.

Since starting his work in wildlife trade, Galster has spearheaded undercover investigations on rhino horn smugglers in southern China, tiger-skin traders in Russia, whale meat smuggling in Japan, and much more. "The trade is huge and diverse," he laments. "My team and I have worked on stopping smugglers trading not only in parts of elephants, bears, whales, and rhinos, but live pangolins, snakes, turtles, lorises, lions—even smugglers that specialize in plants, such as ginseng. I've posed as both a buyer and a seller for scores of animals and plants. And the work is truly inspiring. I see government officials and nongovernment organizations really trying to do something to beat the illicit system, alongside enforcement officers and local people who wanted to see the laws work. This is work that I want to keep doing not only because it needs to be done, but together I think we are making a difference."

MAY BERENBAUM
POLLINATOR DECLINE

"Insects have lived on Earth far longer than humans have, in many more different places, and they've found at least a million different ways to make a living here— we're living on their planet, not the other way around."

FAST FACTS

Pollinator Decline

→ **Issue:** Insect pollinators, specifically bees, have experienced dramatic declines over the past 60 years, with additional devastating crashes just since 2006.

→ **Impact:** Pollinator declines threaten the reproduction of 75 percent of the world's flowering plants and one-third of all food production in the United States.

→ **Trend:** Regional reports of declines vary widely between 30 percent and 90 percent, with some bee-keepers reporting almost complete loss. The 2010 USDA data show overall honey bee losses estimated at 34 percent annually since the appearance of colony collapse disorder.

May Berenbaum

→ **Education:** PhD from Cornell University

→ **Nationality:** American

→ **Organizational Affiliation:** University of Illinois at Urbana-Champaign

→ **Years Working on Addressing Pollinator Decline:** 30+

→ **Honors:** Tyler Prize for Environmental Achievements (2011); Public Understanding of Science Award from the American Association for the Advancement of Science (2010); numerous regional and national distinguished teaching awards from the Entomological Society of America

→ **Books:** *Buzzwords: A Scientist Muses on Sex, Bugs, and Rock 'n' Roll*; *Bugs in the System: Insects and Their Impact on Human Affairs*; *Ninety-Nine More Maggots, Mites, and Munchers*; *The Earwig's Tail: A Modern Bestiary of Multi-Legged Legends*; *Honey, I'm Home-made: Sweet Treats from the Beehive across the Centuries and around the World* (coauthored)

→ **Notable Accomplishments:** Chair of the National Research Council Committee on the Status of Pollinators in North America; entomology department head at the University of Illinois at Urbana-Champaign; founder and organizer of the annual Insect Fear Film Festival; fellow of the National Academy of Sciences, the American Academy of Arts and Sciences, and the American Philosophical Society; former president of the American Institute for Biological Sciences

What You Should Know about Pollinator Decline

→ Fruits and seeds produced by plants requiring insect pollinators are the staple diet of 25 percent of all bird species and an important food resource for many mammals and other wildlife.

→ There are approximately 20,000 species of bees on Earth, which can be found on every continent except Antarctica. Most of these species have been little studied.

→ Colony collapse disorder has been reported in 36 North American states, and similar problems have been seen in many European countries, including Spain, France, Portugal, Belgium, Greece, Italy, the Netherlands, and Ireland. Taiwan has also reported possible cases.

WHEN you've had a TV character named after you—*X-Files* personality and famed entomologist Dr. Bambi Berenbaum—you know you've had an impact. And in fact, that is just what May Berenbaum has had. Berenbaum has brought a unique approach to attracting attention for the most unpopular of Earth's creatures: insects. While a graduate student at Cornell University, Berenbaum envisioned the idea of a film festival where people could learn about, as well as be entertained by, bugs of all species, even those enhanced by animation and computer generation, as well as the imaginations of the filmmakers behind the camera. She instituted her creative, yet initially considered outrageous, idea in 1984 after becoming a professor at the University of Illinois; much to many people's surprise, it was popularly received. The Insect Fear Festival has been a huge success and is still held annually at the school. Berenbaum figures it's all good fun and good publicity for her beloved bugs. "People tend to dismiss all insects as annoying at best and dangerous at worst, assuming we'd all be better off without them," she says. "Truth be told, human life on this planet would likely be, if not impossible, then thoroughly unpleasant without insects."

Insects are responsible for the pollination of 75 percent of the world's flowering plants and fully one-third of the food humans eat—some of the most nutritious foods, at that. Fruits, vegetables, and nuts rely on insect pollination. Bees, flies, wasps, butterflies, and beetles—as well as a few vertebrates, including bats and birds—all contribute to the facilitation of plant reproduction and were doing the job long before humans started getting involved. The Western or European honey bee, *Apis mellifera,* important to Europe's economy, was imported to the United States for honey production in 1621, and other places around the world followed suit. The bees were imported to Central and South America in the eighteenth century, and Australia in the early 1820s. Ever since intensive management of the honey bee began in Europe, they have become the main powerhouse when it comes to agricultural pollination. States Berenbaum, "Honey bees are essentially six-legged livestock—they're the world's premier managed pollinators. Nearly one hundred crop species in the United States depend entirely on pollination services delivered by honey bees, and collectively these crops and uses to which they're put contribute about $15 billion to the economy annually. What's astonishing, however, is how little attention we've paid to this multibillion-dollar business partner." In fact, even the basic nutritional needs of bees have been poorly studied. Commercial hive bees often find only one type of food, as they are placed into artificial agricultural monocultures—just one variety of crop at a time. In winter, bees are often "fed" sugar or high-fructose corn syrup—providing calories, but not satisfying their protein needs. "Bees need proper nutrition as much as people do. Not only so they can work long hours providing pollination services but so that they tend to their own business of raising their offspring and manufacturing honey and wax. That's a lot to ask of anyone being given a junk-food diet," says Berenbaum.

As important as they are to the global economy, bees have had significant threats in modern history. In the mid-1980s, infestations of introduced, parasitic mites became a significant factor in declines. These mites have been controlled to a certain extent with various chemical treatments in managed hives, although some have developed resistance, making control more difficult. More

recent declines of bees, however, are more baffling and harder to contend with.

Berenbaum headed up an ad hoc committee on the status of pollinators for the National Academy of Sciences and reported before a subcommittee of the U.S. House of Representatives Committee on Agriculture. Her committee recommended that more dollars be allocated to research and more information be collected on bee biology and pollination services, not just honey production, which had been the focus in the past. They also warned that reliance on a single species for a majority of our agricultural pollination needs was risky and unsound. The committee was convened, and formed its recommendations prior to the awareness of CCD, or *colony collapse disorder*. "Within a month of the publication of our study," Berenbaum said, "reports started coming in about mysterious disappearances of massive numbers of honey bees;

our warning that the apiculture industry was perilously unstable seemed eerily prophetic. If there is a silver lining to this dark cloud, it's that the federal government and the science community mobilized rapidly to study in unprecedented depth many of the aspects of honey bee biology that had been too long neglected."

First detected in Pennsylvania in 2006, and now with an official name but no official cause, colony collapse disorder has been documented with a 98 percent disappearance of bees in some areas. Theories abound, starting with pesticide use, viruses, and parasites, and continuing on to poor nutrition, depressed immune systems, and/or climate change, but the one thing all scientists know is that they don't know exactly what's going on or why.

Since the first reports of the new pollinator population crash became known, Berenbaum has been investigating factors thought to be responsible for the declines and has begun to piece some

information together. After comparing cells from healthy bees with those that had died from CCD, she found that the CCD bees had likely been affected by multiple viruses at the same time, inhibiting their ability to fight the illnesses.

But honey bees are not the only pollinators in trouble; for many groups of pollinators, a multitude of ecological and environmental challenges seem to be leading to a "death by a thousand cuts." Habitat fragmentation and deterioration, exposure to agricultural pesticides, and competition with invasive species present challenges to pollinators of all descriptions. Changes in geographic distributions of pollinators and the plant species they visit that lead to loss of synchrony, possibly because of global climate change, and to disruption of migratory routes by urbanization and other development, may be responsible for reductions in numbers of hummingbirds, nectar-feeding bats, and some butterflies and moths.

Amid all the struggles to discover the causes of population crashes, Berenbaum sees more than just economic value in pollinators. "Bees are among the most extraordinary animals on the planet; with brains no bigger than a pinhead, they can collectively coordinate the activities of fifty thousand individuals in a hive so that all members are fed, housed, and kept safe from enemies." Bees not only can navigate to and from a food source; they can communicate the precise location of that resource to the rest of the hive via a symbolic "dance language." "That's why figuring out what's causing colony collapse disorder is so difficult," Berenbaum

contends. "Even a slight disruption of the incredibly sophisticated behavior of the honey bee—anything that affects their ability to communicate or navigate—might lead to the collapse of the hive. Most insects just aren't that complicated."

One of Berenbaum's life missions is to increase the world's scientific interest and literacy. Her innovative methods for engaging the public and providing interesting ways to obtain that information led to her being awarded the Public Understanding of Science Award from the American Association for the Advancement of Science in 2010. It is what also motivated Berenbaum to write her general-interest books on insects. "I enjoy the challenge, actually, of piquing people's interest—making them realize they might actually want to learn more about insects." And with a title such as *Buzzwords: A Scientist Muses on Sex, Bugs, and Rock 'n' Roll,* written by a professor with a beloved *X-Files* character named after her, Berenbaum may have figured out how to turn the world's attention to bugs and encourage new ways to look at our relationship with insects and the services they provide. "After all," she says, "insects have lived on Earth far longer than humans have, in many more different places, and they've found at least a million different ways to make a living here—we're living on their planet, not the other way around."

HOW TO HELP

WORKING TOGETHER TO MAKE A DIFFERENCE